CW00686935

WINDOWS WORKSTATION 4 FOR DUMMIES®

Quick Reference
2nd Edition

by Valda Hilley

IDG
BOOKS
WORLDWIDE

IDG Books Worldwide, Inc.
An International Data Group Company

Foster City, CA ✦ Chicago, IL ✦ Indianapolis, IN ✦ New York, NY

Windows NT® Workstation 4 For Dummies® Quick Reference, 2nd Edition

Published by
IDG Books Worldwide, Inc.
An International Data Group Company
919 E. Hillsdale Blvd.
Suite 400
Foster City, CA 94404
www.idgbooks.com (IDG Books Worldwide Web site)
www.dummies.com (Dummies Press Web site)

Library of Congress Catalog Card No.: 98-89936

ISBN: 0-7645-0497-5

Printed in the United States of America

10 9 8 7 6 5 4 3 2 1

2P/RU/QR/ZZ/IN

Distributed in the United States by IDG Books Worldwide, Inc.

Distributed by Macmillan Canada for Canada; by Transworld Publishers Limited in the United Kingdom; by IDG Norge Books for Norway; by IDG Sweden Books for Sweden; by Woodslane Pty. Ltd. for Australia; by Woodslane (NZ) Ltd. for New Zealand; by Addison Wesley Longman Singapore Pte Ltd. for Singapore, Malaysia, Thailand, and Indonesia; by Norma Comunicaciones S.A. for Colombia; by Intersoft for South Africa; by International Thomson Publishing for Germany, Austria and Switzerland; by Distribuidora Cuspide for Argentina; by Livraria Cultura for Brazil; by Ediciencia S.A. for Ecuador; by Ediciones ZETA S.C.R. Ltda. for Peru; by WS Computer Publishing Corporation, Inc., for the Philippines; by Contemporanea de Ediciones for Venezuela; by Express Computer Distributors for the Caribbean and West Indies; by Micronesia Media Distributor, Inc. for Micronesia; by Grupo Editorial Norma S.A. for Guatemala; by Chips Computadoras S.A. de C.V. for Mexico; by Editorial Norma de Panama S.A. for Panama; by Wouters Import for Belgium; by American Bookshops for Finland. Authorized Sales Agent: Anthony Rudkin Associates for the Middle East and North Africa.

For general information on IDG Books Worldwide's books in the U.S., please call our Consumer Customer Service department at 800-762-2974. For reseller information, including discounts and premium sales, please call our Reseller Customer Service department at 800-434-3422.

For information on where to purchase IDG Books Worldwide's books outside the U.S., please contact our International Sales department at 317-596-5530 or fax 317-596-5692.

For information on foreign language translations, please contact our Foreign & Subsidiary Rights department at 650-655-3021 or fax 650-655-3281.

For sales inquiries and special prices for bulk quantities, please contact our Sales department at 650-655-3200 or write to the address above.

For information on using IDG Books Worldwide's books in the classroom or for ordering examination copies, please contact our Educational Sales department at 800-434-2086 or fax 317-596-5499.

For press review copies, author interviews, or other publicity information, please contact our Public Relations department at 650-655-3000 or fax 650-655-3299.

For authorization to photocopy items for corporate, personal, or educational use, please contact Copyright Clearance Center, 222 Rosewood Drive, Danvers, MA 01923, or fax 978-750-4470.

About the Author

Valda Hilley is a computer consultant and author who has written several computer books (among them, *Windows NT Secrets* and *Windows 3.1 Configuration Secrets*) and numerous articles filled with technobabble and secret information. A Windows NT user since its initial release, she demystifies and decodes Windows NT for the rest of the world in *Windows NT Workstation 4 Quick Reference For Dummies,* 2nd Edition.

Acknowledgments

Thanks to IDG Books, Jim McCarter, and the editorial staff at Dummies Press for staying the course.

To my friends at Microsoft, thanks for a helping hand.

ABOUT IDG BOOKS WORLDWIDE

Welcome to the world of IDG Books Worldwide.

IDG Books Worldwide, Inc., is a subsidiary of International Data Group, the world's largest publisher of computer-related information and the leading global provider of information services on information technology. IDG was founded more than 30 years ago by Patrick J. McGovern and now employs more than 9,000 people worldwide. IDG publishes more than 290 computer publications in over 75 countries. More than 90 million people read one or more IDG publications each month.

Launched in 1990, IDG Books Worldwide is today the #1 publisher of best-selling computer books in the United States. We are proud to have received eight awards from the Computer Press Association in recognition of editorial excellence and three from Computer Currents' First Annual Readers' Choice Awards. Our best-selling ...For Dummies® series has more than 50 million copies in print with translations in 31 languages. IDG Books Worldwide, through a joint venture with IDG's Hi-Tech Beijing, became the first U.S. publisher to publish a computer book in the People's Republic of China. In record time, IDG Books Worldwide has become the first choice for millions of readers around the world who want to learn how to better manage their businesses.

Our mission is simple: Every one of our books is designed to bring extra value and skill-building instructions to the reader. Our books are written by experts who understand and care about our readers. The knowledge base of our editorial staff comes from years of experience in publishing, education, and journalism — experience we use to produce books to carry us into the new millennium. In short, we care about books, so we attract the best people. We devote special attention to details such as audience, interior design, use of icons, and illustrations. And because we use an efficient process of authoring, editing, and desktop publishing our books electronically, we can spend more time ensuring superior content and less time on the technicalities of making books.

You can count on our commitment to deliver high-quality books at competitive prices on topics you want to read about. At IDG Books Worldwide, we continue in the IDG tradition of delivering quality for more than 30 years. You'll find no better book on a subject than one from IDG Books Worldwide.

John Kilcullen
Chairman and CEO
IDG Books Worldwide, Inc.

Steven Berkowitz
President and Publisher
IDG Books Worldwide, Inc.

Eighth Annual Computer Press Awards ≥ 1992

Ninth Annual Computer Press Awards ≥ 1993

Tenth Annual Computer Press Awards ≥ 1994

Eleventh Annual Computer Press Awards ≥ 1995

Publisher's Acknowledgments

We're proud of this book; please register your comments through our IDG Books Worldwide Online Registration Form located at: http://my2cents.dummies.com.

Some of the people who helped bring this book to market include the following:

Acquisitions, Editorial, and Media Development

Project Editor: Susan Christophersen

Director of Acquisitions and Product Development: Mary Bednarek

Acquisitions Editor: Joyce Pepple

Technical Editor: Jim McCarter

Editorial Manager: Mary C. Corder

Editorial Assistant: Alison Walthall

Production

Project Coordinator: Valery Bourke

Layout and Graphics: Lou Boudreau, Linda M. Boyer, Angela F. Hunckler, Brent Savage, Kate Snell

Proofreaders: Christine Berman, Kelli Botta, Michelle Croninger, Arielle Carole Mennelle, Nancy Price, Janet M. Withers

Indexer: Donald Glassman

General and Administrative

IDG Books Worldwide, Inc.: John Kilcullen, CEO; Steven Berkowitz, President and Publisher

IDG Books Technology Publishing: Brenda McLaughlin, Senior Vice President and Group Publisher

Dummies Technology Press and Dummies Editorial: Diane Graves Steele, Vice President and Associate Publisher; Mary Bednarek, Director of Acquisitions and Product Development; Kristin A. Cocks, Editorial Director

Dummies Trade Press: Kathleen A. Welton, Vice President and Publisher; Kevin Thornton, Acquisitions Manager

IDG Books Production for Dummies Press: Michael R. Britton, Vice President of Production and Creative Services; Cindy L. Phipps, Manager of Project Coordination, Production Proofreading, and Indexing; Kathie S. Schutte, Supervisor of Page Layout; Shelley Lea, Supervisor of Graphics and Design; Debbie J. Gates, Production Systems Specialist; Robert Springer, Supervisor of Proofreading; Debbie Stailey, Special Projects Coordinator; Tony Augsburger, Supervisor of Reprints and Bluelines

Dummies Packaging and Book Design: Patty Page, Manager, Promotions Marketing

♦

The publisher would like to give special thanks to Patrick J. McGovern, without whom this book would not have been possible.

♦

Table of Contents

Part VII: Reaching Out with Windows Messaging and Outlook Express 87

How to Use This Book

Welcome to the *Windows NT Workstation 4 For Dummies Quick Reference,* 2nd Edition, a guide designed to make life with Windows NT Workstation 4 quicker and easier. This book gives you just what you need to get in and out of Windows NT Workstation 4 and get your work done.

Keep this book at your side for those times when you need quick steps for performing a new task or a handy refresher for a procedure you've forgotten.

How This Book Is Organized

This book is divided into ten parts and a glossary.

Part I: 1, 2, 3, Install Windows NT

There may come a time when you have to install or reinstall Windows NT. Part I shows you how to get through the installation without losing control.

Part II: Getting to Know Windows NT

Part II of this book provides you with the basic information you need to get started, including how to start and quit Windows NT. This part helps you find your way around the desktop, the display area that serves as a launch point for most of your work with Windows NT. Along the way, you discover the commands, menus, and dialog boxes that put you in control of your Windows NT program. If you hit a stumbling block, help is only a mouse click or keystroke away; this part introduces you to the easy-to-use Help program.

Part III: Bringing the Web to Your Desktop with Internet Explorer

Everybody's doing it and you should, too. Windows NT puts the information superhighway, the Internet, in everyone's reach. Part III of this book will quickly show you how to make your desktop look and act like the Web, complete with live content from the Web using the Active Desktop feature.

Part IV: Working with Files and Folders

Part IV explains everything you need to know about organizing electronic files and folders with Windows NT. You find out how to create folders for your files, as well as how to find, open, move, copy, and delete files.

Part V: Networking with Others Near and Far

If you're ready to expand your horizon beyond the realm of your own computer, then Part V is the part for you. In this part, you discover how to connect to computers in your network, connect to printers on your network, and share your printer. You also find out how to browse your workgroup or domain and how to use dial-up networking.

Part VI: Printing for Show and Tell

Want to print your masterpiece? Then turn to Part VI to find out how to print a file. You also find out how to cancel a print job, change printer settings, set a default printer, and more.

Part VII: Reaching Out with Windows Messaging and Outlook Express

Part VII focuses on using both Microsoft's Windows Messaging, which comes with Windows NT, and Outlook Express, which comes with Internet Explorer 4, to communicate with the outside world. You discover how to create and send e-mail messages, as well as print and save your messages. If you want to attach documents to your e-mails, this part provides easy steps.

Part VIII: Using All Those Accessories

Part VIII introduces you to the finer things in life — such as the CD player, Calculator, and games you can play. You also get to experiment with other Windows NT accessories, such as Clipboard Viewer and Notepad.

Part IX: Maintaining Your Computer

In Part IX, you discover how to successfully manage and maintain your system. You find out how to make changes to the system's settings and configurations using several different Windows NT utilities or tools found in the Control Panel.

Part X: Keeping Tabs on Windows NT

Windows NT is a big, powerful operating system that can handle many tasks. One of its most powerful features is the capability to manage multiple users. In other words, you can be the boss. At least you can be the boss of your computer and control how people can use your computer, or access files and printers from your computer. Part X tells you what you need to know to be director of your "computer world" by administrating your computer or network.

Glossary: Techie Talk

There are lots of strange words that people throw around in a Windows NT environment. Techie Talk gives you a clue as to what those geeks are talking about.

The Cast of Icons

This icon alerts you to useful information or helpful shortcuts that make using Windows NT Workstation easier.

To avoid potential problems, read the information marked with this icon and proceed with caution.

This icon flags a common problem associated with a particular task or a feature that may not work as expected.

Read the information marked with this icon to find out the quickest way to accomplish a task.

Do you need more information on a particular topic? This icon points you to a useful section of the book, *Windows NT Workstation 4 For Dummies,* 2nd Edition, written by Andy Rathbone and Sharon Crawford and published by IDG Books Worldwide, Inc.

1, 2, 3, Install Windows NT

Windows NT's install process is fairly straightforward. However, there are many decisions you have to make along the way. Making the wrong decision can cause problems with the installation. This part takes you through the installation process step by step, providing guidelines to help you make appropriate decisions and pointing out paths to help you steer clear of pitfalls.

In this part . . .

✔ **Preparing for installation**

✔ **Overviewing the installation process**

✔ **Installing Windows NT Workstation**

Ready . . . Set . . . Install

Before you install Windows NT Workstation 4.0, you should do the
following:

✦ **Check Hardware Compatibility.** Make sure that the hardware
on which you are installing meets Microsoft's hardware
compatibility tests for Windows NT 4.0 and appears on
Microsoft's Hardware Compatibility List (HCL). Some computers may have peripherals that are not yet supported by
Windows NT Workstation 4.0, or that require a device driver
supplied by the manufacturer. For information regarding the
HCL, refer to www.microsoft.com/hwtes.

✦ **Read the Latest Installation Instructions.** Microsoft is
continually making minor changes even after the product goes
out the door. They document these last minute changes in the
installation notes that are available on the CD. Before installing Windows NT Workstation 4.0, read the setup release notes
(setup.txt) that can be found in the root directory of the
Windows NT Workstation 4.0 compact disc. There are several
other README files in the system32 directory that also
contain last minute changes: readme.wri, network.wri, and
printer.wri.

✦ **Check the domain or workgroup name.** If this computer is to
join an existing domain, you need to know the name of the
domain or workgroup.

✦ **Check your printer.** If you have a printer connected directly
to your computer, record the printer model and port used by
the printer.

✦ **Obtain your OEM drivers.** If you have proprietary or unsup-
ported hardware, you should assemble these driver diskettes
before you begin your installation. During the installation,
Setup gives you a chance to install OEM (Original Equipment
Manufacturer) drivers.

✦ **Check for free disk space.** Windows NT requires about 90 MB
for a complete installation (this includes the minimum paging
file size). If Setup cannot find enough free space on a single
disk drive, the installation program halts, prompting you to
reformat your disk drive in order to continue the installation.
You can always exit the installation by pressing the F3 key,
delete some files, and then restart the installation process.

✦ **Check for compressed files.** If you use the Microsoft
DriveSpace or Microsoft DoubleSpace disk compression utility
to compress files on Windows 95 or MS-DOS, Windows NT
cannot install onto a compressed partition.

✦ **SCSI devices must be on for Setup.** You should ensure that all SCSI devices are on.

✦ **Disconnect UPS serial connections.** UPS serial-monitoring cable connections should be disconnected during Setup. Windows NT attempts to automatically detect devices connected to serial ports, which could cause problems with UPS equipment connected to a serial port.

✦ **Copy third-party drivers to the boot floppy.** If Setup is being run on a system that has a SCSI device installed that is not supported by one of the drivers that ships with Windows NT 4 Workstation, copy the proper Windows NT device driver onto the boot floppy before starting the Setup process.

Smoothing the Road with Upgrading Tips

If you are upgrading from Windows NT Workstation 3.51, some of the device drivers may not work correctly and need to be updated to work with Windows NT Workstation 4.0. Always check with the manufacturer of these devices to make sure that you have the latest drivers.

Also, before installing Windows NT Workstation 4.0, check with your hardware manufacturer to get the latest versions of their machine BIOS, which may have been updated to work with Windows NT Workstation 4.0. Many hardware vendors now provide these online via their Web sites.

Due to system changes, Windows NT Workstation 3.51 video and printer drivers will not work with the 4.0 release.

Windows 95 and Windows NT Workstation may look alike but the differences in their registry architectures make it impossible to upgrade a Windows 95 machine to Windows NT Workstation. If you intend to install Windows NT Workstation on a machine that is already running Windows 95, you must create a new directory and reinstall all of your applications.

Setup at a Glance

At first glance, installing Windows NT Workstation resembles installing Windows 95 or Windows 98. The basic steps when installing Windows NT on a computer for the first time are as follows:

1. Start the Setup program. How you start Setup depends on what kind of hardware you have and whether you are running Setup from floppy disks, a CD-ROM, or a shared network directory.

2. Choose Express Setup.

3. Specify whether you're upgrading an existing Windows NT installation or performing a new installation. If it is a new installation, choose the disk partition, file system, and directory for the Windows NT system files to be installed on your computer.

4. Provide identification information about your user name, computer name, and other identifiers.

5. Choose the local language you want to use.

6. Set up your network adapter card and select the default network protocol.

7. Set up the locally installed printer, if you have one.

8. Set up a password for the administrator's account for the computer.

9. Set the local time, specify video adapter settings, and create an Emergency Repair disk.

Stepping Through Setup

Microsoft went to great lengths to simplify the Windows NT Workstation 4.0 install or upgrade process. Users coming from previous versions of NT will notice the new user interface, improved hardware detection, installation wizards, and a restartable GUI-mode setup. Windows NT Workstation is typically installed using either the boot disks or CD-ROM.

Start the Windows NT Setup process by rebooting the system with the boot disks or CD ROM. NT Setup loads and executes the Windows NT Setup Loader, which in turn executes a program to determine the hardware configuration of the system. During the detection process, Windows NT displays the message `Windows NT Setup is inspecting your computer's hardware configuration`.

Choosing the setup mode

You can choose to do an Express or Custom Setup of Windows NT. Express Setup is the "no brainer" way to install Windows NT. Express Setup asks you the minimum number of questions and installs all optional Windows NT components. It automatically configures your hardware settings and other components. This is the road to take!

Setup probes your system

After choosing Express setup, Windows NT Setup probes your system in an attempt to determine what, if any, SCSI devices exist in the system. It is at this point that Setup allows you to install device drivers from third-party hardware vendors.

Selecting a file system

After you select the partition on which to install Windows NT, Setup gives you the choice of either keeping the existing file system or converting the partition to NTFS (if the partition is currently formatted as FAT).

When bringing up a new system, I recommend that you use the FAT file system initially. This allows you to get the operating system installed and to test network connections from all sides because some operating systems cannot mount NTFS volumes. Also, you can recover from installation errors easier by having the hard disk formatted with a file system that DOS and other Windows versions can easily be installed on. In general, format NT Workstations with FAT (to maintain compatibility with other file systems).

The graphic mode portion of setup

To set up graphic mode:

1. Enter a name and company name. Windows NT uses the names to identify you for various operations.

2. Enter a Product Identification number. Technical support representatives use this number to identify your system. Look for it either on the inside back cover of your Installation Guide or on your registration card.

What's in a computer name?

You must provide a name to identify your computer on the network. This name must be 15 characters or fewer and must not be the same as any other computer name, domain name, or workgroup name on the network.

Don't play games with the computer name

Many people use the names of their favorite characters, cars, or movies as computer names. Although this may provide unique names, it's a strategy that doesn't hold out over long periods and numerous machines. Be conventional when naming computers; use department or division names so that users browsing the network will have an idea of a particular server's function.

What not to use in a computer name

Do not use the characters in the following table in computer names because they can cause unexpected results when the computer is accessed over the network.

Character	Name	Keystroke
*	Bullet	ALT+0149
£	Currency sign	ALT+0164
|	Broken vertical bar	ALT+0166
§	Section sign	ALT+0167
¶	Paragraph sign	ALT+0182

What language do you speak?

Setup next asks for the Language, or Locale, of the system. This information is used for formatting date, time, and currency information.

Printer configuration

Next, you have a chance to set up a default printer. You should do this only if you have a printer attached to the system locally or need to print to non-Windows NT print shares. NT does not require a local printer driver as long as you're printing to a Windows NT print share. If you're setting up to print to a non-Windows NT network printer, temporarily assign that printer to LPT1. After Setup installs the network components, you can redirect printing to the network print share using the Network option.

Network configuration

Under an Express Installation, Windows NT automatically searches for a network card and makes the appropriate selection. With the network card determined, Setup presents a dialog box showing the detected network card's settings: the I/O (input/output) port address, the memory address setting for the card, and the IRQ (interrupt request) setting.

Networking services overview

Next, Setup installs the network services necessary to support the card, default workstation, and server components. After Setup successfully copies these files, it installs the rest of the files necessary for Windows NT and then starts the Network Control Panel applet. The Network Settings dialog box displays the installed network hardware and software configuration information.

Choosing protocols

Windows NT Setup adds the basic software you need to begin working on the network immediately. However, you may want to install additional network services on your Windows NT computer. Network *services* are components that add networking capabilities to Windows NT.

A network *protocol* is a set of rules that allows computers on a network to communicate with each other. Two computers must use the same network protocol (speak the same language) to communicate.

Protocols communicate through other layers of software that control the flow of information. How network protocols and other layers of network software work together is determined by network *bindings*. Windows NT automatically binds network protocols to all appropriate layers.

The following protocols or services are available under NTS:

+ **DLC protocol.** The Data Link Control (DLC) protocol allows access to IBM mainframe computers or printers attached directly to the network.

+ **NetBEUI protocol.** NetBIOS extended-user interface is the standard protocol for the NetBIOS interface; it is for local area networks (LANs) of 20 to 200 workstations.

+ **NWLink IPX/SPX Compatible protocol and Gateway Service for NetWare Networks.** These are the transport protocols used in Novell NetWare networks and the service that allows access to files, directories, and printers on NetWare servers.

+ **TCP/IP and related components.** A suite of Transmission Control Protocol/Internet Protocol (TCP/IP) protocols is used for communicating in heterogeneous, interconnected networks.

Choosing the protocols to use in a network requires evaluating several elements of the network, such as the number and types of computers, special hardware or software used, and compatibility and integration into existing networks.

Administration password

Windows NT Setup asks you to specify a password for the special Administrator user account. This account enables you or someone you designate to log on to the computer with maximum access. Then, if the computer is not joining a domain, Setup asks you to specify the user name and password for a local account.

NT requests this user name and password each time you log on. The user name may have up to 20 characters and contain any upper- or lowercase characters except the following:

" / \ [ ] : | = , + * ? < >

A password can contain up to 14 characters and is case sensitive (for example, Windows NT distinguishes between the passwords Cpress and cpress).

If you lose the Administrator account password for your computer, there is no way to recover it. If no other Administrative accounts have been created, you have to reinstall NT and set a new password to log on as Administrator.

Final stages of setup

When you reach this stage of setup, you're in the home stretch. Setup does the following:

+ Creates Program groups.

+ Creates the Emergency Repair disk, saving the default configuration information (necessary to restore Windows NT) on the Emergency Repair diskette.

+ Sets the system's time zone setting. Unless the system happens to be in the Greenwich mean time zone, you must select the correct time zone.

When Setup is finished running, you get a message asking you to restart your computer. Remove any disks from the floppy disk drives and choose the Reboot button to start NT.

Part II

Getting to Know Windows NT

The road to Windows NT 4 is paved with Windows 3.1, Windows for Workgroups, Windows NT 3.*x*, and Windows 95 or 98. How you use this book depends on your migration path. If you're migrating from Windows 95 or Windows 98, you can probably skip this part — it's old news to you. But if you're new to Windows in any flavor, look in this part for the basics that will make your road to Windows NT 4 smoother.

Most of the Windows NT features are discussed in detail throughout this book, but you need to know the basics in order to work comfortably with those features.

In this part . . .

- ✓ Getting Help
- ✓ Starting and quitting Windows NT
- ✓ Working with dialog boxes
- ✓ Working with menus and commands
- ✓ Moving windows
- ✓ Sizing windows
- ✓ 101 ways to start a program — not!
- ✓ Switching between programs
- ✓ Running programs
- ✓ A bunch more stuff

Associating File Types

Windows NT is smart enough to open a file with the corresponding application as long as you tell it what goes where and why. For example, if you use Microsoft Word for Windows, it creates a file with .DOC as the filename extension. Windows NT can and will open Word for Windows whenever you open a file with the .DOC extension.

To tell Windows NT which application created a document file:

1. In Windows NT Explorer, choose View⇨Options and click the File Types tab.

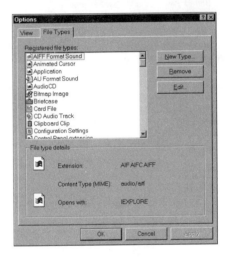

2. Click the New Type command button and use the Add New File Type dialog box to specify which application opens the file type.

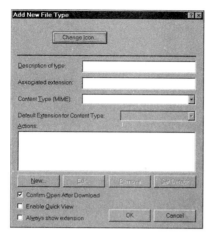

Commands

Commands . . . you give them. You take them. You use commands to instruct programs what to do.

To choose commands:

- ✦ Use the mouse or keyboard to choose commands from a menu or menu bar. *See also* "Menu commands," later in this part.

- ✦ Click buttons on toolbars (where available). *See also* "Toolbars," later in this part.

- ✦ Use the drag-and-drop features to move, copy, and print files or to start applications. *See also* Part II.

- ✦ Double-click icons in a window or on the desktop.

- ✦ Type the name of a command in a Command Prompt window and press Enter.

Creating a Shortcut

The shortest distance between two points is a straight line, also known as a shortcut. Windows NT enables you to create *shortcuts,* which are icons that start a program or open a file. Why a shortcut? You can create multiple shortcuts of a program file, for example, and place the shortcuts in convenient locations, such as on the desktop.

Creating a shortcut from Windows NT Explorer

To create a shortcut from Windows NT Explorer:

1. Open Windows NT Explorer.

2. Select the program for which you want to make a shortcut.

3. Point to the File menu and then point to Create Shortcut. The shortcut appears in the list of files. You can drag the shortcut to the desktop.

To create a shortcut from Windows NT Explorer without first finding the file for which you want to make a shortcut:

1. Open Windows NT Explorer.

2. Point to the File menu, point to New, and then point to Shortcut. The Create Shortcut dialog box appears.

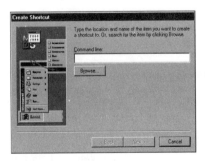

3. Click the Browse button. The Browse dialog box appears.

4. Using the Browse dialog box, locate the file for which you want to make a shortcut. Then double-click the program file.

5. Click the Next button. The Select a Title for the Program dialog box appears.

6. Type a name for the shortcut and then click the Finish button. The shortcut appears in the file list. If you select the wrong program, click the Back button to return to the Browse dialog box instead of clicking the Finish button.

Creating a shortcut from the desktop

To create a shortcut from the desktop:

1. Point to a location on the desktop and right-click the mouse.

2. Point to New and then point to Shortcut. The Create Shortcut dialog box appears.

3. Click the Browse button. The Browse dialog box appears.

4. Using the Browse dialog box, locate the file for which you want to make a shortcut. Then double-click the program file.

5. Click the Next button. The Select a Title for the Program dialog box appears.

6. Type a name for the shortcut and then click the Finish button. The shortcut appears in the file list. If you selected the wrong program, click the Back button to return to the Browse dialog box instead of clicking the Finish button.

Placing a shortcut in the Start menu

To place a shortcut in the Start menu:

1. Create a shortcut as described in the preceding section.

2. Drag the shortcut to the Start menu. The shortcut appears at the top of the Start menu.

Desktop

When you start Windows NT, you see a large display area called the *desktop.* You can compare the desktop to a conventional desk on which you place the items you work with throughout the day. The desktop is the starting point for most of your interaction with Windows NT.

As you survey the desktop, you see the following items depending on the Windows NT components you have installed:

What You See	What It Is	What It's For
	My Computer	You can use My Computer to quickly and easily see everything on your computer. Double-click the My Computer icon on the desktop to browse through your files and folders.
	Network Neighborhood	If you are using a network, the Network Neighborhood icon appears on your desktop. Double-click it to browse through the computers in your workgroup or domain and the computers on your entire network.
	Inbox	Microsoft Exchange provides a universal inbox that you can use to send and receive electronic mail. In addition, you can use the inbox to organize, access, and share all types of information, including faxes and items from online services.

What You See	*What It Is*	*What It's For*
	Briefcase	The Briefcase is a really cool tool that helps you keep files up-to-date when you use two computers, such as your office computer and your portable computer.
	Recycle Bin	When you erase files, Windows NT Explorer doesn't just remove them from your disk. If you're erasing files from a hard disk, Windows NT Explorer moves the files to a special type of folder called the Recycle Bin so that you can retrieve the files later if you want. As a part of regular housecleaning, you need to empty the Recycle Bin to delete the files and reclaim valuable hard disk space.
Start	Start button	At the bottom of your screen is the Taskbar. It contains the Start button, which you can use to quickly start a program or to find a file. When you open a program, document, or window, a button appears on the Taskbar. You can use this button to quickly switch among the open windows.
	Shortcut icons	Windows NT 4 lets you add icons for commonly used programs, documents, folders, and other items to the desktop. If these icons appear on your desktop, you can launch a program or open a document or folder by double-clicking it.

Dialog Boxes

A dialog box is simply an on-screen form that you fill out to tell Windows NT how to process a command. Any time Windows NT needs information on how to proceed, a dialog box asks for certain information. Any time you see a menu command followed by an ellipsis, you know that a dialog box appears when you choose that command.

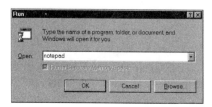

If Windows NT requires more information or a decision from you, the dialog box has command buttons.

 Windows NT often displays messages or warnings in the guise of a dialog box. Sometimes the dialog box is simply a message informing you of possible consequences of a command action. To dismiss a message, click OK. If the message contains two or more command buttons, click OK to proceed or click Cancel to cancel the action and dismiss the message.

Making selections

To make selections within a dialog box:

1. Select options or type text to specify the information you want in a dialog box.

Click an option to select it or press Alt plus the underlined letter in the option name. If an item in a dialog box is dimmed, it is unavailable because it requires a selection or some previous action.

 If you don't know what an option does, press F1 or click the Help button to see a description of the options.

2. When you finish with the dialog box, choose the appropriate command button to carry out the command.

Usually, clicking OK carries out the command. Sometimes the button that carries out the command has a label such as Open or Find Next.

The following list presents guidelines for using buttons and other items in dialog boxes.

When you choose option buttons and check boxes:

✦ Click an option button to select it and to turn off any other option in the group. You can select only one option button in a group.

✦ Click a check box to turn that option on or off. You can select as many check boxes as you want.

A selected option button contains a dot, and a selected check box contains a check mark.

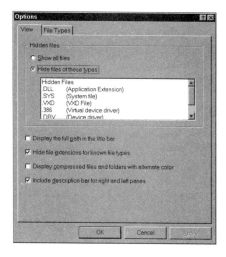

When you choose command buttons:

+ Another dialog box appears if you choose a button with an ellipsis.

+ The dialog box expands if you choose a button with double arrows.

When you choose list boxes:

+ Click an item in any kind of list to select it or scroll to see more items.

+ In a drop-down list box, click the arrow to display a list of options to select.

+ In some lists, you can select multiple items. In such a list, click a selection a second time to turn it off.

When you choose a item, you can type, edit, and paste text in any text box. If a text box contains text when you move to it, all the text is selected and any text you type replaces it. You can also press Delete or Backspace to delete any unwanted text and type any changes.

Closing a dialog box

To close a dialog box, try one of the following methods:

+ Click Cancel.

+ Click the Close button (the X button in the upper-right corner of the dialog box).

+ Press the Esc button.

Explorer

Windows NT Explorer lets you do a couple of things: It lets you view everything that is on or attached to your computer, and it lets you work with files stored on your hard disk and other parts of your system. Windows NT Explorer contains the following items:

Icon	Description
	Represents your desktop. If you click the desktop icon, Windows NT Explorer uses the file pane to show everything on your desktop — including any shortcut icons.
	Represents your computer, including its disks, printers, and any system folders for fonts and Control Panel settings.
	Represents a hard drive. If you click the hard drive icon, Windows NT Explorer displays folders and files on the hard drive.
	Represents a folder. If the folder is selected, it appears open. Otherwise, the folder appears closed. If the folder has subfolders within it, Windows NT Explorer places a plus sign (+) in front of the folder.
	Represents an application file. You can start the application by double-clicking it or by selecting it and choosing the File⇨Open command.
	Represents an associated data file. You can launch the application along with the data file by double-clicking it or by selecting it and then choosing the File⇨Open command.
	Represents an unassociated data file. You cannot open these kinds of files by double-clicking them because Windows NT doesn't recognize what kinds of files they are. Instead, you choose the File⇨Open With command to tell NT what program to use to open the file.
	Represents a CD-ROM drive. If you click a CD, Windows NT Explorer shows the files and folders located on that CD.
	Represents your computer's fonts. If you click the Fonts folder, Windows NT Explorer shows all the fonts installed on your computer.
	Represents the Control Panel. If you click the Control Panel folder, Windows NT Explorer shows the Control Panel applets used to alter and maintain your computer's settings.
	Represents the printers available to your computer. If you click the Printers folder, Windows NT Explorer shows the printers connected to your computer or available over the network.
	Represents the network your computer is attached to. If you click the Network Neighborhood folder, Windows NT Explorer shows the computers, and their respective folders and files, connected to your network.

Icon	Description
	Represents the Recycle Bin. If you click the Recycle Bin folder, Windows NT Explorer shows the files and folders you have erased.
	Represents another computer that you can access remotely. If you click the Dial Up Networking icon, the computer sets itself up for remote access. (The Dial Up Networking item will not be present if you have not installed the Dial Up Networking software.)
	Represents your Briefcase. The Briefcase folder is a special folder where you can synchronize copies of files. You can, for example, copy files from a network drive to your Briefcase. Then you can modify the files in the Briefcase and synchronize them so that the copies on the network drive are updated automatically. This feature is great for notebook computers that travel with files that need updating.

Help — How to Get It

Online help is only a mouse-click or keystroke away from wherever you are in Windows NT. When in doubt, simply look up the topic in Help. You can access help by selecting Help from the menu bar in any window, pressing F1, or choosing Help from the Start button.

The following table shows what you can do (and how you can do it) in the Help window:

What You Can Do	How You Do It
Go back to a previous topic	Click the Back button or click the Help Topics button to return to the Contents tab of Help and select another subject. If a Display History window appears in Help, you can select a previous help item from the History window.
Jump to another Help topic	Click the underlined jump term. You can also click the Help Topics button and then select another topic. Many Help windows have a Related topics button at the end of the Help text that you can click for information on related items, too.
Display a definition	Click the term with the dotted underline and then click anywhere on-screen to close the definition.
Minimize Help to an icon	Click the Minimize button in the Help window.
Exit Help	Click the Close button.

Customizing a Help window

You can customize the Help window in many ways. For example, you can select the font size or colors used to display Help, and you can make the Help window always stay on top of other windows.

To change the font of the Help window:

1. From the Help window, click the Options button.

2. Select Font. Another menu appears.

3. Select the size of the font — Small, Normal, or Large.

To change the colors:

1. From the Help window, click the Options button.

2. Select Use System Colors to toggle between the default Help window colors and the system colors that you have defined for all windows. If a check mark appears in front of the Use System Colors option, Help is currently displaying Help windows using the default system colors.

A dialog box appears, asking "For the color change to take effect, Help must be restarted. Do you want to close Help now?"

3. To accept your change, click Yes. Of course, clicking No in this dialog box returns you to the Help window.

To make Help always stay in front of other windows:

1. From the Help window, click the Options button.

2. Select Keep Help on Top. Another menu opens.

3. Select On Top to always keep the Help window on top or Not On Top to prevent Help from staying on top of other windows. If you select Default, Help follows the parameters defined by the program for which you are displaying Help.

Finding a topic in Help

To find a topic in the Windows NT Help system, try one of the following methods:

✦ Click the Contents tab to see topics by category.

✦ Click the Index tab to see a list of entries. You can either type the word you're looking for or scroll through the list of entries.

✦ Click the Find tab to search for words or phrases.

Getting information on dialog box settings

To get Help on each item in a dialog box:

1. Click the question-mark button at the top of a dialog box.

   (If the dialog box doesn't have the button, look for a Help button or try pressing F1.)

2. Click the item you want information about. A pop-up window appears.

3. If you want to print or copy the information in a pop-up window, right-click inside the window and then click <u>P</u>rint Topic.

4. To close the pop-up window, click inside it.

Another way to get Help on an item on-screen is to use your right mouse button to click the area that you want Help on and then click the <u>W</u>hat's This? command.

Getting help for MS-DOS commands

To get help on an MS-DOS command, type the name of the command you want Help on at the command prompt, followed by /?. For example, type **format /?** to get Help on the Format command. You can also type **Help** and the command you want help on. For example, enter **Help Format.**

To stop the screen from scrolling too fast and to display Help text one screen at a time, type the command followed by | more. For example, type **format /?** | **more** for Help on the Format command. To scroll to the next screenful of text, press any key.

Personalizing a Help topic

When you *annotate* a Help topic, you add additional information to the Help topic. If a Help topic has an annotation, a paper clip appears next to its title. To view the annotation, you just click the paper clip.

To annotate a Help topic:

1. From a Help window, click the <u>O</u>ptions button.

2. Select <u>A</u>nnotate. The Annotate window opens.

3. Type the additional information you want to remember about this Help topic.

4. Click the Save button. You can also click the Delete button to erase the annotation, the Copy button to copy the annotation information to the clipboard, or the Paste button to paste information into the annotation box.

Printing a Help topic

To print a Help topic, try one of the following methods:

✦ In the Help topic you want to print, click the Print button or the Options button (which button appears depends on where you have accessed Help from) and then click Print Topic.

✦ Simply right-click inside the Help window and then click Print Topic on the pop-up menu.

You can print a group of related topics by clicking the appropriate book icon in the Help Contents windows and then clicking Print.

To print the Help in a pop-up window, use your right mouse button to click inside the pop-up window and then click Print Topic.

Searching for Help with Find

To search for a topic by using the Find dialog box:

1. In the Help Topics window, click the Find tab to display the Find options.

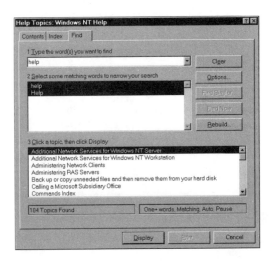

2. In the Find dialog box, type the word or phrase you're looking for.

3. Select a word or phrase that matches the topic you're searching for.

4. In the bottom list box, click the topic titles that are relevant to your search and then click the Display button to view the topic.

Beginning a new search

To begin a new search, click the Clear button in the Find dialog box.

Specifying the settings to use with Find

To specify the settings to use with Find:

1. Click the Options button in the Find dialog box to display the Find Options dialog box.

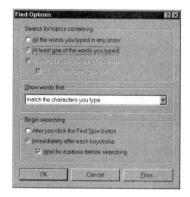

2. Click the corresponding option button in the Search for Topics Containing box to indicate how you want to search for a topic. You can search for topics containing

• All the words you typed in any order

• At least one of the words you typed

3. Select the desired setting in the Show words that list box. You can set the Find dialog box to show words that

• Begin with the characters you type

• Contain the characters you type

• End with the characters you type

• Match the characters you type

4. In the Begin Searching box, click one of the following option buttons to tell Find when to begin searching:

- After you click the Find Now button

- Immediately after each keystroke

To search the index for Help topics:

1. In the Help Topics window, click the Index tab.

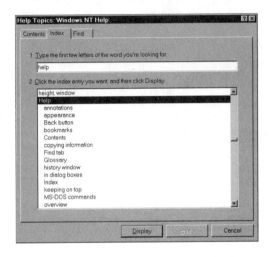

2. In the Index dialog box, type the first few letters of the word you're looking for.

3. Click the desired index entry and then click the Display button.

Starting Help

To start Help, try one of the following methods:

◆ Press F1 wherever you are working.

◆ Click the Start button on the Taskbar and then click Help.

In either case, the Help Topic: Windows NT Help dialog box appears. The Help Contents window lists the major topics for Windows NT. From this window, you can move to more specific information by clicking the Contents, Find, or Index tabs. To see a list of index entries in any tab, either type the word you're looking for or scroll through the list.

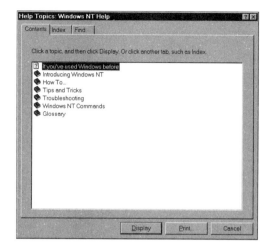

Using the Help Contents

When the Help system first starts, the Help Topics: Windows NT dialog box appears with the Contents tab showing. The Contents tab displays the table of contents for the Help system in sections represented by icons that look like books.

To open a book:

1. Click the book.

2. Click the Open button to view the topics in the book.

To view a topic:

1. Click the topic.

2. Click the Display button.

Icons

The desktop can hold a lot of different elements, many of which appear as an icon of some sort. An icon is nothing more than a picture that represents something else. In Windows NT and Windows-based applications, icons represent things like applications, folders, shortcuts, and documents. (*See also* "Desktop," earlier in this part.)

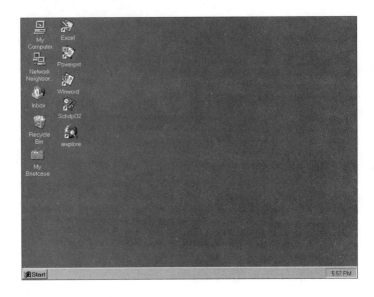

Menu Commands

All Windows-based applications group commands into sets called
menus, which are displayed in the menu bar across the top of the
application window. Menus vary in each application, but most
applications include at least a File menu, Edit menu, and Help
menu.

To choose a menu command:

1. Choose the menu name in the menu bar and hold down the
mouse button.

2. Drag to select the command you want and then release the
mouse button.

You can also activate the command by pressing the Alt key and the
underlined letter in the menu name.

Control menu commands

Control menu commands appear on the Control menus of application windows, document windows, and some dialog boxes.

To activate the Control menu of a window or dialog box, click the Control menu button located in the upper-left corner of the window or dialog box.

The Control menu commands let you manipulate a window or dialog box in the following ways:

Click This Command	*To Do This*
Restore	Undo the last Minimize or Maximize command.
Move	Tell Windows NT that you want to move the application window. When you click this command, the pointer changes to a four-headed arrow. You move the window by using the cursor direction keys on your keyboard to indicate the direction in which you want the window to move. Press Enter when finished.
Size	Tell Windows NT that you want to change the size of the application window. When you click this command, the pointer changes to a four-headed arrow. You change the window size by using the cursor direction keys on your keyboard to extend or shrink the window's border. Press Enter when finished.
Minimize	Tell Windows NT that you want to remove the application window from the screen. Windows NT hides the application window and leaves its icon on the Taskbar as a reminder that the application is active.
Maximize	Tell Windows NT that you want the application window to expand and fill up the entire screen.
Close	Close the window and, consequently, the application itself. If you close a document window, you also close the document. If you haven't saved the document, you may lose your work. Most applications ask, however, whether you want to save the document or file before closing it.

The commands available on the Control menu vary for different applications, but most Control menus include at least the <u>M</u>ove and <u>C</u>lose commands.

Shortcut menus

Shortcut menus are a new feature that found their way first into Windows 95 and now into Windows NT 4. The idea is that many applications have enough intelligence to know what commands are needed in a given situation. Some applications are so smart that they know which commands you will most likely need in a situation.

To display a shortcut menu, right-click the object you want to manipulate. Then click the desired command from the shortcut menu.

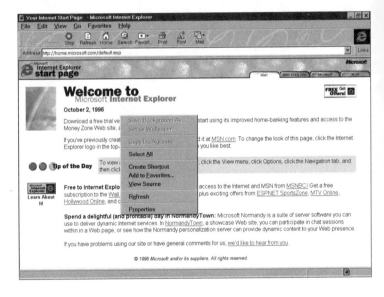

For example, if you right-click an object, the menu that appears shows the most frequently used commands for that file or folder.

Quitting MS-DOS

To quit MS-DOS, type **exit** at the command prompt, or click the close box.

Running Programs by Double-Clicking

If you double-click a document on the desktop or in Windows NT Explorer, Windows NT opens the application and then tells the application to open the document file — if Windows NT knows which application created the document.

Running Programs by Using the Find Command

Your computer's hard drive or your company network is a vast storage system where files and programs can hide.

To run programs by using the Find command:

1. Click the Start button. The Start menu appears.

2. Point to Find to display the menu.

3. Click Files Or Folders to display the Find: All Files dialog box.

4. In the Named box, type all or part of the filename.

If you do not know the name of a file or want to refine the search, click the Date Modified or Advanced tabs.

If you want to specify where Windows should begin its search, click the Browse button to select a folder where you want the search to begin.

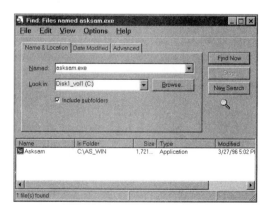

5. Click the Find Now button to begin the search.

6. Double-click the program file to start the program.

Running Programs by Using the Run Command

If there's no program shortcut on the desktop and you know the name of the program you want to run, the Run command is a quick and easy route.

To run programs by using the Run command:

1. Click the Start button. The Start menu appears.

2. Click Run to display the Run dialog box.

3. In the Open box, type the location and name of the program you want to start.

4. Click OK or press Enter.

If you don't remember the location or name of the program file, click the Browse button.

To select a program you started recently, click the down arrow in the Open box, click a program in the list, and then click OK.

You can open a file or folder or connect to a shared computer by typing its path in the Open box.

Running Programs by Using the Start Button

Certainly the easiest — and perhaps the most obvious — way to start a program is to use the Start button.

To start a program by using the Start button:

1. Click the Start button. The Start menu appears.

2. Point to Programs. The Programs menu appears, listing program names or folders.

3. Click the program you want to start. If the program you want is not on the menu, point to the folder on the menu that contains the program and then click the program you want to start.

If the program you want to start doesn't appear on the Programs menu or one of its submenus, use the Find command on the Start menu, as described in "Running Programs by Using the Find Command," earlier in this part.

Running Programs from Windows NT Explorer

Microsoft designed the Windows NT Explorer to replace Program Manager and File Manager, so it makes perfect sense that you can run a program from Windows NT Explorer.

To run a program from Windows NT Explorer:

1. Click the Start button. The Start menu appears.

2. Point to <u>P</u>rograms.

3. Point to Windows NT Explorer.

You also can run a program from Windows NT Explorer by using these two methods:

✦ Double-click the My Computer icon, select a drive icon, and then choose <u>F</u>ile➪<u>E</u>xplore.

✦ Right-click the My Computer icon and select <u>E</u>xplore from the shortcut menu.

When you select a program, if the folder containing the program is not active (its icon appears as a closed folder), scroll through the file pane until you see the program's filename and then double-click the program file.

Scroll Bars

Scroll bars are usually found along the right side and bottom edge of an application window. Scroll bars let you move the window's contents up and down and side to side so that you can see a document or data that's too long or wide to fit entirely within the window.

To use the mouse to manipulate the scroll bar, choose one of the following methods:

✦ Click the arrow at either end of the scroll bar to move in the direction of the arrow.

✦ Grab the scroll box and drag it in the direction you want to move.

✦ Simply click on the scroll bar above or below the scroll box in the direction that you want the window to move.

Selecting Stuff

In a Windows World, you must specify an object (disk, file, folder) for a command to act upon. Simply put, you have to point out the object of your desire.

Selecting disks

To select a disk, click the disk icon.

Selecting files

To select a file, make sure that the folder containing the file is active (appears open). Scroll through the file pane until you see the file and then click the file.

You can select multiple files by clicking the first file and then pressing the Shift key while you click the last file. This action selects a group of contiguous files. If you need to select a random group of files, hold down the Ctrl key and select one file at a time.

Selecting folders

To select a folder, scroll through the folder pane until you see the folder and then click the folder.

If the folder is a subfolder in another folder, you may need to expand the parent folder by double-clicking it in order to select the subfolder.

Shutting Down

Stop! Don't touch that power switch until you read this section. Windows NT must be allowed to shut down gracefully.

To shut down your computer:

1. Click the Start button. The Start menu appears.

2. Click Sh<u>u</u>t Down. The Shut Down Windows dialog box appears.

3. Click the Shut Down the Computer? radio button, then click OK.

4. Do not turn off your computer until a message appears telling you that it is now safe to turn off your computer.

Start Menu

The Start menu appears when you click the Start button.

You can add or remove items from the Start menu or its submenus.

What's on the Start menu?

Icon	Function
Programs	Displays the Programs menu, which lists any Programs submenus including the MS-DOS Prompt and Windows NT Explorer.
Documents	Displays a list of up to the last 15 documents you've used. You can open any of the documents on the list by simply clicking the document's name.
Settings	Displays the Settings submenu, which contains the following menus:
	Control Panel: Displays the Control Panel applet.
	Printers: Displays the Printers window so that you can add a new printer, modify an existing printer, or view documents being printed.
	Taskbar: Displays the Taskbar Properties dialog box so that you can change the way the Taskbar works.
Find	Displays the Find submenu.
	Files or Folders: Displays the Find: All Files dialog box so that you can search for files or folders.
	Computer: Displays the Find: Computer dialog box so that you can search for computers on a network.
Help	Displays the Help Topics window so that you can get help with commands and procedures.
Run	Displays the Run dialog box, which you can use to start programs.
Shut Down	Displays the Shut Down dialog box so that you can exit Windows NT.

Adding programs to the Start menu or Programs menu

To add a program to the Start menu or Programs menu:

1. Click the Start button. The Start menu appears.

2. Point to Settings.

3. Click Taskbar and then click the Start Menu Programs tab in the Taskbar Properties dialog box.

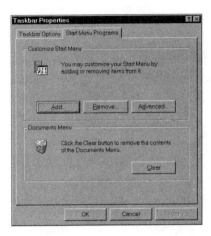

4. Click the Add button and then click the Browse button in the Create Shortcut dialog box.

5. Locate the program you want to add in the Browse dialog box and then double-click it.

6. Click the Next button to display the Select Program Folder and then double-click the menu on which you want the program to appear.

7. In the Select a Title for the Program dialog box, type the name that you want to see on the menu and then click Finish.

Clearing documents from the Documents menu

To clear the contents of the Documents menu:

1. Click the Start button. The Start menu appears.

2. Point to Settings.

3. Click Taskbar and then click the Start Menu Programs tab.

4. In the Documents Menu area, click the Clear button.

You can replace Steps 1, 2, and 3 by right-clicking the taskbar and selecting Properties. Then click the Start Menu Programs tab.

Removing programs from the Start menu

To remove a program from the Start or Programs menu:

1. Click the Start button. The Start menu appears.

2. Point to Settings.

3. Click **T**askbar and then click the Start Menu Programs tab.

4. Click the **R**emove button and then locate the program you want to remove.

5. Click the program and then click the **R**emove button. Confirm your action by selecting yes or no in the Confirm File Delete dialog box. Although this action deletes the shortcut from the Start menu, the original program remains on your computer.

Starting an MS-DOS Program

To start an MS-DOS program, type the name of the program file at the command prompt in the MS-DOS Prompt window and press Enter.

To start an MS-DOS window:

1. Click the Start button. The Start menu appears.

2. Point to Programs on the menu. The Programs menu opens.

3. Click Command Prompt to display the MS-DOS Prompt window.

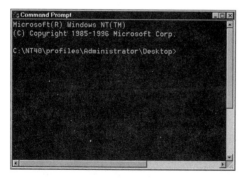

4. Type the directory path and the name of the program file and press Enter.

To switch between a full screen and a window, press Alt+Enter.

Starting Programs Each Time Windows NT Starts

To start a program each time Windows starts:

1. Click the Start button. The Start menu appears.

2. Point to Settings on the menu.

3. Click Taskbar to display the Taskbar Properties dialog box.

4. Click the Start Menu Programs tab.

5. Click the Add button and then click the Browse button to display the Browse dialog box.

6. Locate the program you want to start and then double-click it.

7. Click the Next button and then double-click the StartUp folder.

8. Type the name of the program that you want to see on the StartUp menu and then click the Finish button.

If Windows prompts you to choose an icon, click one and then click the Finish button.

Starting Windows NT

Unlike DOS or other versions of Windows, Windows NT is a secure system — to log on successfully, you must get past NT's first line of defense, the Welcome box. You must identify yourself and enter a password each time you start Windows NT.

To start Windows NT:

1. Turn on your computer.

2. If your computer is set up to start more than one operating system, press an arrow key at the startup screen to choose Windows NT and then press Enter.

3. When the logon message appears, press Ctrl+Alt+Delete to log on.

The Ctrl+Alt+Delete sequence ensures the security of your system. Even if you see a message already displayed that asks you to enter your password, always press Ctrl+Alt+Delete before you type your password.

4. In the Logon Information dialog box, type your username and password.

If you're starting Windows NT for the first time and do not already have a password, simply enter a password and confirm it by entering it again when Windows NT asks.

5. Select either your local computer name or the name of a Windows NT Server domain.

6. Click OK.

As soon as you log on, you can run applications, share files with other users on the network, connect to a printer, and control who has access to your computer and its files.

Starting Windows NT Explorer

Although you won't see an icon for Windows NT Explorer sitting on your desktop, you can get to the Windows NT Explorer without leaving your desktop.

To start Windows NT Explorer, choose one of the following methods:

✦ Click the Start button. The Start menu appears. Point to Programs and then point to Windows NT Explorer.

✦ Double-click the My Computer icon, select a drive icon, and then choose File⇨Explore.

✦ Right-click the My Computer icon and then choose Explore.

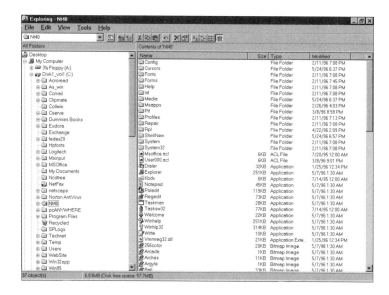

Switching between Programs

When you start a program, a button representing the program appears on the Taskbar. Before you can switch between applications, you must, of course, have multiple applications running.

To start a new application or another instance of an application:

1. Click the Start button. The Start menu appears.

2. Point to Programs. The Programs menu appears, listing program names and folders.

3. Click the program you want to start. If the program you want is not on the menu, point to the folder on the menu that contains the program.

To switch from application to application after they're running, simply click the application button on the Taskbar. Or press and hold the Alt key and then press the Tab key to toggle from application to application. When the application you want to use appears, release the Alt key.

Taskbar

The Taskbar lives at the very bottom of your screen, although you can move it to another position. The Taskbar holds the Start button and buttons for any applications that are running. You can move, stretch, shrink, or even hide the Taskbar.

Moving the Taskbar

The Taskbar lives at the bottom edge of your screen by default. You can move it to the top, right, or left edge of the screen if you like.

To move the Taskbar, grab the Taskbar and drag it to its new location.

Resizing the Taskbar

To resize the Taskbar:

1. Position the mouse cursor over the edge of the Taskbar until the pointer changes to a double arrow.

2. Drag the edge of the Taskbar to stretch it or shrink it.

Hiding the Taskbar

To hide the Taskbar:

1. Click the Start button. The Start menu appears.

2. Point to Settings.

3. Click Taskbar.

4. Make sure the Auto Hide box is checked.

To redisplay the Taskbar, point to the area of your screen where the Taskbar is located. The Taskbar reappears and remains visible until you click another application or move the mouse to another area of the screen.

Note: When hiding the Taskbar, make sure that the Always on top check box is checked. This way, the Taskbar pops up over a maximized application rather than behind the application.

Title Bars

Title bars tell you what application you're currently running and the name of the document showing in the document window. (This is really handy if you forget what program you're working in and what it is that you're working on.)

Toolbars

Toolbars are the rows of buttons, boxes, or tools that sometimes appear immediately beneath an application's menu bar. Toolbar buttons provide shortcuts for activating certain menu commands. To activate a Toolbar shortcut, simply click the button.

Using the Mouse

Windows NT often requires you to use the mouse in different ways depending on the task at hand. You can click, double-click, right-click, or drag.

Clicking

Clicking is probably the mouse action you'll use the most. To click means that you point at an object and click the left mouse button. (If you're left-handed and have your mouse set up so that the right mouse button is the primary button, then click the right button.)

Double-clicking

Double-clicking means to click the primary mouse button two times — fast. You need a steady hand to master this action because you have to click twice without moving the mouse.

Right-clicking

Right-clicking means to point to an object and click the right mouse button (the left mouse button for you lefties who have the right button set as the primary button). Right-clicking is the same action as clicking, just a different button and a different result. Usually, a shortcut menu pops up when you right-click an object.

Dragging

Drag means to point to an object, press and hold the primary mouse button, and then move the mouse to move the object to another location.

Windows Buttons

Look around the edges of a Windows-based program, and you see buttons and icons. You use buttons and icons to display the Control menu (see the Control menu commands in this part), to close an application, and to minimize or resize an application's window.

Click This Button	To Do This
Program button	Display the application's Control menu
Document button	Display the document's Control menu
Minimize button	Shrink a window down to an icon on the Taskbar
Restore button	Restore a window to its previous size
Maximize button	Enlarge a window to fill the screen
Close button	Close the application and any documents opened within the application

Part III

Bringing the Web to Your Desktop with Internet Explorer

Your desktop can come alive with the Active Desktop interface that allows you to pull content (stuff) from Web pages, or a channel (kind of like a TV channel), on your desktop. Some people like to keep tabs on their money so that they can put a stock ticker somewhere on their desktop and receive constant updates. If newspapers are your thing, you can turn your favorite online newspaper into your desktop wallpaper. In fact, your desktop can truly be your own space or gateway to the world by adding the active items such as news, weather, sports, stock prices, or whatever. It's your desktop — let it show!

In this part . . .

- ✓ **Installing Active Desktop**
- ✓ **Turning Active Desktop on**
- ✓ **Using channels**
- ✓ **Viewing Web pages on your Active Desktop**
- ✓ **Using a Web page image as desktop wallpaper**

Active Desktop

Using the Active Desktop feature to keep on top of news and events is a nice way to manage time in a busy day. No need to thumb through gobs of magazines and papers — just look at your desktop.

Installing Active Desktop

To install Active Desktop:

1. On the Start menu, point to Settings and then click Control Panel.

2. Double-click Add/Remove Programs.

3. Click Microsoft Internet Explorer and then click Add/Remove.

4. Click Add Windows Desktop Update from Web site.

If you do not see this option, then the new desktop is already installed.

If you decide later that you do not want to use this feature, you can follow the same steps to remove it.

Turning Active Desktop on

Make sure you have the Active Desktop installed in order to use the Active Desktop features. If you did not originally install the new desktop, see "Installing Active Desktop," earlier in this part.

1. Right-click the desktop and point to Active Desktop.

2. Make sure View as Web Page is selected.

You can also turn the Active Desktop interface on or off by clicking the Start button, pointing to Settings, pointing to Active Desktop, and then clicking View as Web Page.

Adding Web content to your desktop

You can add any *active content* (news, sports, stocks, and so on) that you want from the Web to your desktop. You can add an item from the Active Desktop Gallery, a page you've seen on the Web as you surfed, or a channel.

To add Web content to the desktop:

1. Right-click the desktop and then click Properties.

2. Click the Web tab. Make sure the View my Active Desktop as a Web page option is checked and then click New.

3. If you want to browse the Active Desktop Gallery for a component to add, click <u>Y</u>es.

4. If you want to select some other Web site, click <u>N</u>o and then type the address of the Web site you want, or click <u>B</u>rowse to locate it.

 You can also right-click any link on a Web page, drag it to the desktop, and then click Create Active Desktop item(s) Here on the menu.

Using a Web page image as desktop wallpaper

To make a Web page your desktop wallpaper:

1. Right-click the desktop and then click P<u>r</u>operties.

2. Click the Background tab.

3. Click <u>B</u>rowse. The Browse dialog box opens.

4. Click the HTML document you want, then click Open to close the Browse dialog box.

5. Click <u>A</u>pply on the Background tab.

The wallpaper appears on your desktop as tiled, stretched, or centered, depending on the current setting in the Display box.

 You can also right-click any graphic on a Web page and then click Set as Wallpaper. The graphic then appears as background on your desktop.

Channels

A *channel* is a Web site designed to deliver content from the Internet to your computer, similar to subscribing to a favorite Web site or cable TV service. Unlike cable TV, you don't have to subscribe to the site to view the content. With channels, the site owner can suggest a schedule for your subscription, or you can customize it yourself. Also, with a channel, you don't see just a Web page — you also get a map of the Web site, which enables you to quickly select and view the content you want.

Displaying the Channel bar on the desktop

You can use the Channel bar to quickly open Web sites from your desktop without first opening the browser.

To display the Channel bar on the desktop:

1. Click the Start menu, point to <u>S</u>ettings, point to <u>A</u>ctive Desktop, and then click <u>C</u>ustomize my Desktop.

2. On the Web tab, select the <u>V</u>iew my Active Desktop as a Web page check box.

3. Select the Internet Explorer Channel Bar check box.

To close the Channel bar, rest your mouse pointer at the top of the Channel bar, and then click the Close button (the small X in the upper-right corner) that appears.

Displaying a channel as a screen saver

Some channels offer some of their content as a screen saver. However, not all channels or channel content is available as a screen saver.

1. Right-click your desktop and then click P<u>r</u>operties.

2. Click the Screen Saver tab.

3. In the <u>S</u>creen Saver list, click Channel Screen Saver.

4. Click Settings and then choose the se<u>t</u>tings you want.

Part IV

Working with Files and Folders

Files and folders, folders and files. They go hand in hand. Whether you know it or not, you create them every time you work with your computer. They come from your word processor, your spreadsheet program, e-mail, and Internet programs. Through-out the course of your day you create more documents and data files than you care to count. As files begin to proliferate and accumulate, knowing how to care for them becomes more and more important. In this part, you find out how to do important things to your files, like deleting, renaming, copying, and moving them.

In this part . . .

- ✔ **Changing file and folder names**
- ✔ **Making copies of your files**
- ✔ **Creating folders to hold your files**
- ✔ **Removing unwanted files and folders**
- ✔ **Finding files**
- ✔ **Moving files and folders to safe places**
- ✔ **Opening files**
- ✔ **. . . and much more**

Associating File Types

To change which program starts when you open a file, ***see also*** "Associating File Types" in Part II.

Changing a File or Folder Name

One of the best features of Windows is that it allows you to give files meaningful names. No more XK1PFO.DOC! Now you can call the file what it is, as in "My Million Dollar Proposal." If you don't like the name you give it, you can change it.

To change the name of a file or folder:

1. In My Computer or Windows NT Explorer, click the file or folder that you want to rename. You do not need to open it.

2. Choose File⇨Rename. The current file or folder name appears highlighted. Or, right-click the file and choose Rename from the menu.

3. Type the new name (up to 255 characters, including spaces) and then press Enter.

Copying Files or Folders

One file is never enough. Your boss wants a copy, your best friend needs a copy, and so on. Even more important is that *you* need a copy. If you remember only one thing from this section of the book, remember the word *backup*. No, I don't mean work in reverse. I mean keep duplicate copies of your important files.

To copy files, you use Windows NT Explorer. ***See also*** Part I.

Using the mouse to drag and drop a copy

To copy a file or folder by using the mouse:

1. In Explorer, click the disk drive icon of the drive that contains the file or folder you want to copy.

2. If you want to copy the folder and its entire contents, click the folder. If you want to copy a file or files within a folder, click the file in the Explorer file pane.

3. Drag the folder or file to the disk drive icon to which you want to copy the folder or file.

To copy a file or folder to another folder on your hard disk by using the mouse:

1. Click the disk drive icon of the drive that contains the file or folder you want to copy.

2. Click the file or folder that you want to copy. If you want to copy the folder and its entire contents, click the folder. If you want to copy a file or files within a folder, click the file in the Explorer file pane.

3. Hold down the Ctrl key.

4. Drag the folder or file to the folder to which you want to copy the file.

Using the menu to copy a file or folder

To copy a file or folder by choosing Edit⇨Copy and Edit⇨Paste:

1. Click the disk drive icon of the drive that contains the file or folder you want to copy.

2. Click the file or folder you want to copy. If you want to copy the folder and its entire contents, click the folder. If you want to copy a file or files within a folder, click the file in the Explorer file pane.

3. Copy the file or folder by choosing Edit⇨Copy.

4. Open the folder or disk where you want to put the copy.

5. Paste the file or folder by choosing Edit⇨Paste.

To select more than one file or folder to copy, hold down the Ctrl key and then click the items you want.

Copying a file to a disk

To copy a file or folder to a disk by choosing File⇨Send To:

1. Click the file or folder that you want to copy. If you want to copy the folder and its entire contents, click the folder. If you want to copy a file or files within a folder, click the file in the Explorer file pane.

2. Choose File⇨Send To. Explorer displays a list of floppy drives on your computer.

3. Click the drive you want to copy the file to.

Making a copy of a disk

To copy a disk using My Computer:

1. Insert a disk in the disk drive.

2. Open My Computer on your Desktop and click the icon for the disk you want to copy.

3. Choose File⇨Copy Disk.

4. Click the drive you want to copy from and the drive you want to copy to, and then click Start.

Sending files to other places

You can send a file to a disk drive, an e-mail program, a fax program, the Desktop, the Briefcase, and a slew of other places, depending on what kinds of application programs you have on your system. And you can do so quickly and painlessly with the Send To command.

To quickly send files to another place:

1. Use your right mouse button to click the file you want to send.

2. Point to Send To, and then click the destination.

Want more destinations? You can add other destinations to the Send To command. In the Send To folder, located in your Windows folder, create shortcuts to the destinations you send files to often — a printer, fax, or particular folder, for example.

Creating Folders

Just like the cardboard file folders that you cram paper documents into at your desk, folders on your Windows NT Workstation desktop help to organize and manage data, software, and other files on your computer system.

To create a new folder:

1. In My Computer or Windows NT Explorer, select the disk drive or open the folder in which you want to create a new folder.

2. Choose File⇨New⇨Folder. The new folder appears with the temporary name New Folder.

3. Type a name for the new folder and then press Enter.

Deleting a File or Folder

If your productivity were measured by the number of documents and files you create on any given day, you'd probably be in line for a huge pay increase. Chances are that your boss would discover that your productivity quotient was way too high and you would be asked to clean out old and unused documents or files to make room for "real" work. To erase a file or folder, you use Explorer. *See also* Part II.

To erase a file:

1. In Explorer, click the file or folder that you want to delete. If you want to delete a folder and its entire contents, click the folder. If you want to delete a file or files within a folder, click the file in the Explorer file pane.

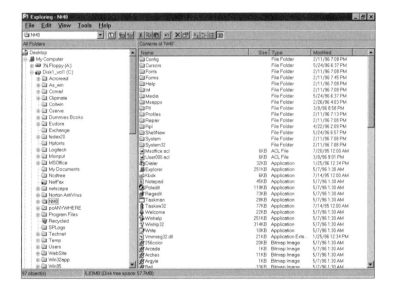

2. Choose File⇨Delete. The Confirm File Delete message box appears.

3. When Windows NT Explorer asks, confirm that you do want to delete the file or folder. Windows NT Explorer then deletes it. If the file is on a hard disk, Windows NT also places it in the Recycle Bin.

See also "Recycle Bin," later in this part.

Permanently removing files when you delete them

In the old days, pressing the Delete key could send you into a serious state of panic if you had your cursor parked over the wrong folder or file. Fear not! Windows NT Workstation has a safety net called the Recycle Bin. Instead of sending files to never-never land when you hit delete, Windows NT moves the files to the Recycle Bin, where they continue to live in a dormant state on your hard disk.

To make sure that the Recycle Bin is ready to recycle:

1. Using your right mouse button, click the Recycle Bin icon on the desktop, and then point to P̲roperties on the menu.

2. Make sure that the Do not move files to the R̲ecycle Bin check box is unchecked.

If you have no fear and like to work without a net, you can set the Recycle Bin so that it does not hold onto files when you delete them.

To actually remove files from your hard disk:

1. Using your right mouse button, click the Recycle Bin icon on the desktop and then point to P̲roperties on the menu.

2. Make sure that the Do not move files to the R̲ecycle Bin check box is selected.

Note, however, that if this box is selected, you are unable to recover any files you delete.

Files deleted from network locations or diskettes, zip disks, and so on are not copied to the Recycle Bin. Windows NT permanently removes them when you delete them. (*See also* "Recycle Bin," later in this part.)

Retrieving deleted files or shortcuts

Oops is a word that I say three or four times a day while working at my computer. You can and will at some point commit an Oops and delete a file that you didn't mean to delete. The good news is that you can get the file back if you have the Recycle Bin activated.

To retrieve a file or shortcut from the Recycle Bin:

1. Double-click the Recycle Bin icon on the desktop.

2. Click the file or shortcut that you want to retrieve.

3. Choose F̲ile⇨R̲estore.

Finding a File or Folder **55**

> If you restore a file that was originally located in a deleted folder,
> Windows recreates the folder and then restores the file to it.

Finding a File or Folder

You know that you're creating them. Sure, they're on your hard
drive, but can you find them? And find them you must because
before you can copy them, delete them, move them, or rename
them, you have to be able to find them. Under Windows NT
Workstation, there must be 50 ways (actually about 5 ways) to find
a file or folder.

Using the Find command

To find a file or folder using the Find command on the Start menu:

1. Click the Start button. The Start menu appears.

2. Point to Find to display the Find submenu.

3. Choose Files or Folders from the menu. The Find: All Files
dialog box appears.

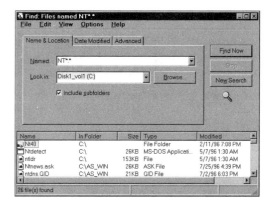

4. In the Named box, type all or part of the filename. Don't panic
if you do not know the name of a file; you can refine the search
by clicking the Date Modified or Advanced tabs and specifying
the appropriate information.

If you want to specify where Windows should begin its search,
click Browse to display the Browse for Folder dialog box and
select the folder where you want to begin the search.

5. Click Find Now to begin the search.

Saving search results

If you find yourself searching for the same files or types of files again and again, you can save the search results:

1. Search for files as described in "Finding a File or Folder," earlier in this part.

2. If you want to save the results of a search along with the search criteria, click Options and then click Save Results.

If you want to save only the search criteria, make sure that the Save Results box is clear.

3. Choose File➪Save Search. Windows NT places an icon representing the search results or search criteria on your desktop.

After you double-click the search results icon, you can restart the search or update the search results by clicking Find Now.

Listing Files in Explorer

Every now and then you need to see what's on your computer. After all, you work so hard creating all those files, and seeing them there on that hard drive is reassurance that your work is not in vain. Besides, who really trusts the computer to store a life's work? Explorer will show you everything if you ask it. To see where the files are, along with their names and extensions and the hierarchy in which they reside, open Explorer and . . . explore.

You can use Explorer to view directories and filenames.

Viewing files

To view a list of files:

1. Start the Windows NT Explorer.

2. Select the disk drive containing the files or directories you want to view.

3. Select the directory containing the files or directories you want to view.

Sorting files

You can sort the files that you are viewing in different ways. To sort a list of files or directories:

1. In Explorer, select the drive and directory you want to view.

2. Choose the View menu.

3. Point to Arrange Icons. A submenu appears.

4. From the submenu, choose the desired way to sort the list of files or directories. Your choices are as follows:

- By Name
- By Type
- By Size
- By Date

Or, in Explorer, click the column heading that you want to use to sort. For example, to sort by date, click the Modified column heading.

TIP

If you set Explorer to show files as large or small icons, Auto Arrange appears as an option on the View⇨Arrange Icons menu. Selecting this option allows Explorer to automatically arrange the icons for display.

Viewing a file's properties

Each file has properties. *Properties* are things such as the date and time the file was created, when the file was last accessed or changed, and other information. You can also change attributes of a file (for example, you can make the file a read-only file).

To view a file's properties:

1. Open Windows NT Explorer.

2. Select the file whose properties you want to view.

3. Open the File menu and then choose Properties. The Properties dialog box for that file appears.

At least two tabs appear in the file's Properties dialog box: the General tab and the Version tab.

The General tab displays the filename, the file type (such as an application), the file location, and the file size. Also displayed in this tab is the MS-DOS name (which is important if the file has a long name) and the date that the file was created, modified, or accessed last. The tab also lists four attributes that you can modify for the file. These are Read-only, Hidden, Archive, and System.

Other tabs that display in this dialog box vary from file to file. For example, if you are viewing the properties of a program file, you view the Version tab.

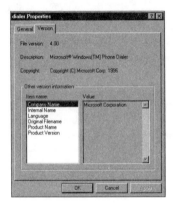

If you are viewing the properties of a graphic file, such as a bitmap file, the tab that you need is the Image tab. With this tab, you can preview the file.

Each type of file that you view the properties for may render different tabs.

Moving Files or Folders

When you want to reorganize files or folders, you'll usually move them.

You use Windows NT Explorer to move files. *See also* Part I.

Using the mouse

To move a file or folder to another folder on your hard disk by using the mouse:

1. In Explorer, click the disk drive icon of the drive that contains the file or folder that you want to move.

2. Click the file or folder you want to move. If you want to move a folder and its entire contents, click the folder. If you want to move a file or files within a folder, click the file in the Explorer file pane.

3. Drag the folder or file to the folder on the hard drive to which you want to move the folder or file.

Using menu commands

To move a file or folder by using menu commands:

1. In Explorer, click the disk drive icon of the drive that contains the file or folder you want to move.

2. Click the file or folder that you want to move. If you want to move a folder and its entire contents, click the folder. If you want to move a file or files within a folder, click the file in the Explorer file pane.

3. Choose Edit⇨Cut.

4. Click the disk drive icon of the drive to which you want to move the file or folder.

5. Click the folder to which you want to move the file.

6. Choose Edit⇨Paste.

Opening a File

Flexibility is the key to gaining oneness with Windows NT. You'll find that it's very flexible, allowing you to be flexible, too. Sometimes you'll launch an application program, such as your favorite word processor, and then use it to open a file to work on. Other times, you may find the file itself in your sights and want to open your word processor with that file as the active document. This is what I call the "outside in" approach. Very flexible.

To open a file from Explorer:

1. In Explorer, click the disk drive icon of the drive that contains the file you want to open.

2. Click the file you want to open.

3. Choose File⇨Open to open the file.

You can also double click the file to open it.

Quick View

Not sure that this is the file you want to work with? No problem. You don't have to open the file to see what's in it. You can get a quick view of what's inside the file right from the Desktop or within Explorer. Simply click a file that you would like to view in My Computer or Windows Explorer and then choose File⇨Quick View.

Or you can right-click the document you want to view and choose Quick View from the shortcut menu.

If you don't see the Quick View command on the File menu, either you don't have a file viewer available for that type of file or Quick View is not installed on your computer.

Quick View has its own command menu:

To Do This	Follow These Instructions
Change the way the document appears	Choose the Page View command on the View menu in Quick View to view the document in pages
Preview a document	Right-click the document and then choose on the desktop Quick View.
Preview another document	Drag the document's icon into the Quick View window.
Edit the document	Choose File⇨Open File for Editing.

Recycle Bin

The Recycle Bin is a welcome sight for those users who often delete the wrong files or simply decide that they want to make use of a file that's been deleted. The Recycle Bin works only with files deleted from Windows NT Explorer.

Emptying the Recycle Bin

To empty the Recycle Bin:

1. Double-click the Recycle Bin icon on the desktop.

2. Choose File⇨Empty Recycle Bin.

If you want to remove only some of the items in the Recycle Bin, hold the Ctrl key while clicking each item. Then choose File⇨Delete.

Changing the Recycle Bin's size

1. Using your right mouse button, click the Recycle Bin icon on the desktop and then choose Properties from the menu. The Recycled Properties dialog box appears.

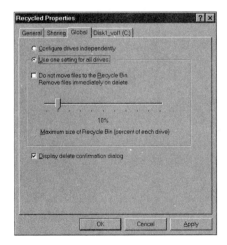

2. Click the Global tab (if your system is set to use one setting for all drives) or click the Disk tab to set the size for that particular disk.

3. Drag the slider control to increase or decrease the amount of disk space that is reserved for storing deleted files.

If you want to use different settings for different drives, select the Configure drives independently option button and then click the tab of the drive whose settings you want to change.

If you want to use the same settings for all drives, select the Use one setting for all drives option button.

Part V

Networking with Others Near and Far

Windows NT is built to network. Although you can use NT as a single or stand-alone computer, odds are that you'll want to connect to another computer in some form or fashion. Whether it's the computer in the next office or a computer on the other side of the world, Windows NT can make the connection.

In this part . . .

✔ **Browsing your Network Neighborhood**

✔ **Connecting to computers in your network**

✔ **Setting up your computer to use a network**

✔ **Using Dial-Up Networking**

Browsing Your Workgroup or Domain

To see what's on your network:

1. Double-click the Network Neighborhood icon. The Network Neighborhood window displays, showing you the computers in your workgroup or domain.

2. Double-click the Entire Network icon in the Network Neighborhood window to view computers in other workgroups and domains.

You can also use the Start menu to see what's on your network:

1. Click the Start button. The Start menu appears.

2. Point to Programs on the Start menu.

3. Click Windows NT Explorer.

4. Click the Network Neighborhood icon to see a list of computers on your network.

To see what drives are accessible on any network computer, click the My Computer icon.

If you are using the Windows NT Explorer, you can see what drives you're connected to by looking in the left window pane for the drives that appear.

Connecting to Computers in Your Network

To view files and directories on computers in your network:

1. Double-click the Network Neighborhood icon on the desktop. You should see the Entire Network icon, which looks like a globe, as well as other computers in your workgroup or domain.

2. If the computer you want to attach to is in another network, double-click the Entire Network icon to display all the networks and domains accessible to your network.

3. Double-click the icon for the computer you want to connect to. A window appears, listing the shared resources for that computer.

4. Double-click the icon for the shared directory that you want to connect to. A window appears, showing the contents of that shared directory. If you get a message saying Access is denied, then you do not have permission to use the share. Contact the administrator of the computer you are connecting to.

Check out *Windows NT Workstation 4 For Dummies,* 2nd Edition by Andy Rathbone and Sharon Crawford (IDG Books Worldwide, Inc.), for more information on networking.

Connecting to Printers on Your Network

To connect to a printer on your network using the Network Neighborhood icon:

1. Double-click the Network Neighborhood icon. The Network Neighborhood window opens.

2. Double-click the computer whose printer you want to connect to. A window for that computer opens, displaying shared resources on that computer.

3. Right-click on the printer resource shown in the window. A menu appears.

4. Select Install from the menu. An icon for that printer is created in your Printers folder.

To install a printer and connect to a printer on your network:

1. Click the Start button. The Start menu appears.

2. Point to Settings on the Start menu.

3. Click Printers on the menu. The Printers folder opens.

4. Double-click the Add printer icon.

5. When the Printer Wizard appears, choose the network printer option and follow the instructions.

See also Part VI for more information on printing.

Dial-Up Networking

Over land, over sea, and even into cyberspace, the Windows NT Dial-Up Networking feature allows you to connect to far-away computers or networks.

To use Dial-Up Networking:

1. Double-click the My Computer icon on the desktop. The My Computer window appears.

2. Double-click the Dial-Up Networking icon. The Dial-Up Networking dialog box appears.

From the Dial-Up Networking dialog box, you can do a number of things. You can:

+ Select the network to dial from the Phonebook entry to dial drop-down list box and then click Dial.

+ Click the <u>N</u>ew button to add a new entry.

+ Click the <u>M</u>ore button to display a menu of more options.

+ View the phone number that you are dialing in the Phone number preview.

+ Before dialing, select a location that you are dialing from in the Dialing fr<u>o</u>m drop-down list box.

If you have not installed Dial-Up Networking, double-clicking the Dial-Up networking enables you to install it. Click the Install butto and then follow along with the Installation Wizard.

Changing dialing settings

To change dialing settings for a Dial-Up connection:

1. Double-click the My Computer icon. The My Computer window opens.

2. Double-click Dial-Up Networking. The Dial-Up Networking dialog box appears.

3. From the Phonebook entry to dial, select the connection whose settings you want to change.

4. Click the <u>M</u>ore button. The More menu opens.

5. Select <u>E</u>dit entry and modem properties from the menu. The Edit Phonebook Entry dialog box appears.

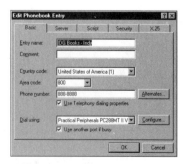

Notice that the Edit Phonebook Entry contains five tabs, shown in the table following these steps.

6. Make all changes necessary and then click OK.

What's This Tab	What You Can Do in the Tab
Basic	Change the Entry name, the comment, the country code, area code and phone number, and the modem to use for dialing. Use the Alternates button to enter more than one phone number to dial. Use the Configure button to configure the modem.
Server	Change the Dial-Up server type and the network protocols you are using. Also, if you are dialing another Windows NT computer, control whether you use software compression. Using software compression can greatly increase the amount of data you can transmit. If you use software compression, do not use modem compression.
Script	Select whether you use a manual or an automated logon. If you are dialing an Internet service provider, for example, you have to enter a user ID and password for validation. You can create a script to enter this information automatically.
Security	Select the level of security to use when transmitting authentication information — either clear text, encrypted authentication, or Microsoft encrypted authentication.
X.25	Enables you to define information for connecting to an X.25 network — a special kind of telephone network set up for data communications. If you don't know what X.25 is, you probably don't need to use this tab.

Creating a location

If you travel with your computer, you will from time to time dial to a computer system from very different locations. For example, if you dial from a motel room, you may have to dial an 8 before dialing the phone number. If you are at home, then you may have to dial *70 to disable call waiting for that one call. If you travel to a place that is long distance from the computer you are dialing, you have to include 1 and the area code, and you may want to include your calling-card number. All these examples are reasons to create a different location.

To create a location, follow these steps:

1. Double-click the My Computer icon on the desktop. The My Computer window appears.

2. Double-click the Dial-Up Networking icon. The Dial-Up Networking dialog box appears.

3. Double-click the icon representing the online connection for which you want to create a location.

4. Click the Dial Properties button in the Connect to dialog box. The Dialing Properties dialog box appears.

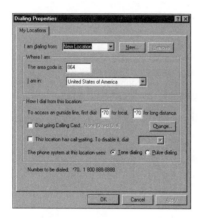

5. Click the Ne̲w button next to the "I am dialing from" list box. The Create New location dialog box appears. Type a name for this new location and click OK to return to the Dialing Properties dialog box.

6. In the The Area C̲ode Is box, type the area code for this location.

> The area code is for where you will be, not the area code of the computer you are dialing.

7. In the I̲ Am In drop-down list box, select the country you will be in.

8. Type the access codes you must use for local or long-distance calls in the for local and for long distance boxes. When you type this code, use a comma to indicate a two-second pause, allowing time for a dial tone. For example, if you have to dial 9 for local calls and 8 plus 1 for long-distance calls, type the following:

9, for local

8,1 for long distance

9. If you use a calling card, check the Dial u̲sing Calling Card check box. Then click the C̲hange button. The Calling Card dialog box appears.

- Select the type of card you use from the Calling Card to use drop-down list box.

- Type your calling card number in the Calling Card number box.

- Click OK.

10. If this location has call waiting and you want to disable call waiting when you place a call, check the This location has call <u>w</u>aiting check box. Then select the code used to disable call waiting from the To disable it, dial drop-down list box.

11. Choose either the <u>T</u>one dialing or <u>P</u>ulse dialing option button.

12. Click OK when you are finished.

Notice that at the bottom of the dialog box, you can see the phone number you are creating.

Creating a network connection

To set up a network connection by using Dial-Up Networking:

1. Double-click the My Computer icon on the desktop. The My Computer window appears.

2. Double-click the Dial-Up Networking icon. The Dial-Up Networking dialog box appears.

3. Click the <u>N</u>ew button. The New Phonebook Entry Wizard appears.

4. In the Name the new phonebook <u>e</u>ntry box, type the name you want to call this connection.

5. Click the <u>N</u>ext button. The Server dialog box appears.

6. Choose all of the following check boxes that apply to your dial-up situation.

- <u>I</u> am calling the Internet.

- <u>S</u>end my plain text password if that's the only way to connect.

- <u>T</u>he non-Windows NT server I am calling expects me to type login information after connecting or to know TCP/IP addresses before dialing.

If you are dialing another Windows NT computer, check only the second check box. If you are dialing the Internet, check at least the first check box and maybe even the third check box.

7. Click the <u>N</u>ext button. The Phone Number dialog box appears.

8. Select the Country code to use and then type the area code and phone number.

9. Click the Next button. The New Phonebook Entry Wizard dialog box appears again. Click the Finish button.

You may want to modify the connection that you just created. If you do, then from the Dial-Up Networking dialog box:

1. Ensure that the correct connection is selected in the Phonebook entry to dial drop-down list box.

2. Click the More button.

3. Choose Edit entry and modem properties.

If you have not created a connection before, a dialog box appears, indicating that the phonebook is empty. When you click OK, the New Phonebook Entry Wizard dialog box immediately appears.

After you have connected to another computer, you can see files and folders on that computer only if they are shared.

Setting Up to Connect to a Network

Most of the time, you set up a computer to use the network during installation. In case you didn't set up the networking features during the initial setup, you can install networking features now using the Network tool in Control Panel.

To set up your computer to use a network:

1. Click the Start button. The Start menu appears.

2. Point to Programs on the Start menu.

3. Click Control Panel to open the Control Panel.

4. Double-click the Network icon.

5. When the Setup Wizard appears, follow the instructions to set up your computer for networking.

Sharing Your Files or Folders on the Network

To share a folder with other members of your network:

1. Find and select the folder that you want others to have access to.

You can use either My Computer or Explorer to locate the folder.

2. Choose File⇨Sharing to display the Properties dialog box for that folder. The Sharing tab is the current tab.

3. Click the Shared As option button.

4. In the Share Name box, type the name to share the directory as or accept the default name.

5. (Optional) Type a description of the share in the Comment box.

6. Select either the Maximum Allowed option button to allow an unlimited number of users to access the share. Or select the Allow option button and type a specific number of users in the Users box to limit the number of users who can access your share.

7. Click the Permissions button. The Permissions dialog box appears.

8. Make any changes to permissions as needed. Click OK when you're finished. You return to the Properties dialog box for the folder you are sharing.

- Click Add to add other permissions.

- Select a permission group and select a different type of access from the Type of Access drop-down list box — choose Full Access, Change, Read, or No Access.

- Select a permission group and click Remove to remove a permission group.

- In most instances, you will assign the Everyone group to have Change permissions.

9. Click OK to complete the sharing.

Sharing Your Printer

To share your printer with others on your network:

1. Double-click the My Computer icon. The My Computer window appears.

2. Double-click the Printers folder. The Printers window appears.

3. Select the printer that you want to share.

4. Choose File⇨Sharing to display the Properties dialog box for that printer. The Sharing tab is the active tab.

5. Select the Shared option button.

6. Type the name for the shared printer in the Share Name box or accept the default name.

7. Click OK. The printer icon appears with a hand under it, indicating that the printer is shared.

To stop sharing, repeat Steps 1–4. Then select the N<u>o</u>t Shared option button and click OK.

During the printer installation process, you have the option to share the printer at that time.

Part VI

Printing for Show and Tell

Computers are supposed to help reduce the amount of paper you need to manage in your life, right? On the contrary; computers give you the power to create more paper faster. And create you will. Now that you've got hoards of information in the computer, this part tells you how to print.

In this part . . .

- ✔ Canceling a print job
- ✔ Changing printer settings
- ✔ Printing a document
- ✔ Viewing a document in print queue

Canceling a Print Job

You can stop the printing of all documents on a printer that is attached to your computer. If you're using a network printer, however, you can cancel only your own documents, unless you have been granted rights to control a printer.

To cancel printing of a document:

1. Click the Start button. The Start menu appears.

2. Point to Settings on the menu. The Settings menu appears.

3. Click Printers. The Printers folder appears.

4. Double-click your printer's icon to display the printer's status dialog box.

5. In the list of jobs being printed, click the document that you want to cancel.

6. Choose Document⇨Cancel.

If the print job that you select to cancel is one that is currently printing, cancellation takes a little longer than if you are canceling a document that is not yet printing. You should pause the printer before canceling the document being printed.

When you cancel a print job, all other print jobs move up in order.

Canceling All Print Jobs

You may, at times, need to cancel all print jobs that are currently set to print on your printer. If you're using a network printer, however, you can cancel only your own documents, unless you have been granted rights to control a printer.

To cancel printing all documents:

1. Click the Start button. The Start menu appears.

2. Point to Settings on the menu. The Settings menu appears.

3. Click Printers. The Printers folder appears.

4. Double-click your printer's icon to display the printer's status dialog box.

5. Choose Printer⇨Purge Print Documents.

All documents that are in line to be printed are removed. You should pause a printer before performing this task.

A quick way to purge all print documents is to perform Steps 1 through 3, right-click the printer whose properties you want to change, and choose P__u__rge Print Documents from the menu that appears.

Changing Printing Order

If you need to print documents in a certain order, you change the order of documents sitting in the print queue.

To change the order of documents in a print queue:

1. Click the Start button. The Start menu appears.

2. Point to __S__ettings on the menu. The Settings menu appears.

3. Click __P__rinters. The Printers folder appears.

4. Double-click your printer's icon to display the printer's status dialog box.

5. Click the document that you want to move and then drag it to its new position in the queue.

 You cannot move a document that is in the process of printing.

Changing Printer Settings

You can alter the printer properties in the Printers folder to set options for all the documents you print on a printer.

To change printer settings:

1. Click the Start button. The Start menu appears.

2. Point to __S__ettings on the menu. The Settings menu appears.

3. Click __P__rinters. The Printers folder appears.

4. Double-click your printer's icon to display the printer's status dialog box.

5. Choose __P__rinter⇨P__r__operties to display the Printer Properties dialog box.

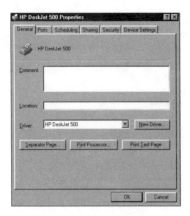

 The settings that you can change depend on the printer type. Click the different tabs to see all the options you can set.

 A quick way to open the Properties dialog box is to perform Steps 1 through 3 and then right-click the printer whose properties you want to change, and choose Properties from the menu that appears.

Changing the printer port

To change the port a printer is connected to:

1. Click the Start button. The Start menu appears.

2. Point to Settings on the menu. The Settings menu appears.

3. Click Printers. The Printers folder apppears.

4. Click your printer's icon.

5. Choose Printer⇨Properties to display the Properties dialog box.

6. Click the Ports tab.

7. You can make a number of changes in this tab.

- In the Print to the following ports area, select another port that you are attaching the printer to by clicking the port's check box.

- Click the Add Port button to add a port that the printer attaches to. When the Printer Ports dialog box appears, select the type of port to add.

- Select a port that you want to delete and click the Delete Port button.

- Select a port and click the Configure Port button to change a port's configuration.

Changing paper size or layout

To change the paper size or layout for printing:

1. Click the Start button. The Start menu appears.

2. Point to Settings on the menu.

3. Click Printers. The Printers folder appears.

4. Click your printer's icon to select the printer.

5. Choose Printer⇨Properties to display the Properties dialog box.

6. Click the Device Settings tab to specify the settings you want. Select the paper size by using the Form To Tray Assignment.

TIP

Your printer may have other Device Settings listed. Scroll through the list to see what adjustments you can make on your printer. For example:

✦ If your printer has memory and you install additional memory, change the memory amount by using Installed Memory.

✦ Select the font cartridge assignment by using Font Cartridge Slot 0 (or other Font Cartridge Slot numbers).

Setting graphics and color options

To set printing options for graphics and color:

1. Click the Start button. The Start menu appears.

2. Point to Settings on the menu.

3. Click Printers. The Printers folder appears.

4. Click your printer's icon to select the printer.

5. Choose Printer⇨Properties to display the Properties dialog box.

6. Click the Device Settings tab.

7. Select Halftone Setup in the list of device options. The Halftone Setup button appears at the bottom of the dialog box.

8. Click the Halftone Setup button to display the Device Color / Halftone Properties dialog box.

9. Make the appropriate changes in this dialog box and then click OK to return to the Properties dialog box for the printer. Click OK again to close the Properties dialog box.

Device Color and Halftone Properties vary from printer to printer.

Checking Print Status

Sending a document to the printer can sometimes be like sending it to no man's land. You can use Print Manager to see where the document went and what's happening to it.

To view printing status after you print a document, a printer icon appears on the Taskbar; double-click that icon to see a list of documents waiting to print.

When your document is finished printing, the printer icon disappears.

Creating a Printer Shortcut

You can create a shortcut of your printer and place the shortcut on the desktop. By doing so, you can easily drag documents for printing to the printer. To create a printer shortcut:

1. Open the Printers folder.

2. Right-click the printer for which you want to make a shortcut.

3. Choose Create Shortcut. A dialog box asks whether you want to place the shortcut on the desktop.

4. Click the Yes button.

Deleting Documents from Print Queue

A print queue is a list of documents waiting to be printed on the printer. In the print queue, you can see information, such as the document's size, its sender, and its printing status.

To stop the print process and delete all the documents waiting to be printed from the print queue:

1. Click the Start button. The Start menu appears.

2. Point to Settings on the menu. The Settings menu appears.

3. Click Printers. The Printers folder appears.

4. Double-click your printer's icon to open Print Manager.

5. Select Printer⇨Purge Print Documents to clear all documents from the print queue.

You cannot remove documents that you did not print from the print queue of a network printer unless you have been given full access to that printer.

Inserting a Banner Page

If you share your printer with a group of people, you may want to use a cover sheet, or *banner page,* to separate your print jobs.

To separate your print jobs with a banner page:

1. Click the Start button. The Start menu appears.

2. Point to Settings on the menu. The Settings menu appears.

3. Click Printers. The Printers folder appears.

4. Right-click the printer you are using to select the printer.

5. Click Properties to open the Properties dialog box for your printer.

6. On the General tab, click the Separator Page button.

7. Click the Browse button to select a document for the separator page.

8. Select the separator page file and then click Open.

9. Click OK to close the Separator Page dialog box and then click OK again to close the Properties dialog box for your printer.

Windows NT includes three separator files: Pcl.sep, Pscript.sep, and Sysprint.sep.

+ **Pcl.sep** switches the printer to PCL printing (a printing language specific to HP printers) and prints a page before each document.

+ **Pscript.sep** switches the printer to PostScript printing, but does not print a separator page before each document.

+ **Sysprint.sep** prints a page before each document. Use this page only for Postscript printers.

Pscript.sep and Sysprint.sep are compatible with PostScript printers.

You can create your own document to use as a separator page.

Installing a New Printer

Before you install a printer, make sure it's attached to the computer and that you know the following:

+ What parallel port the printer is attached to (LPT1, LPT2, and so on)

+ The manufacturer of the printer

+ The printer model

+ The printer driver software if supplied by the printer's manufacturer

To install a new printer:

1. Click the Start button. The Start menu appears.

2. Point to Settings on the menu. The Settings menu appears.

3. Click Printers. The Printers folder appears.

4. Double-click the Add Printer icon. When the Add Printer Wizard dialog box appears, select the My Computer printer option on Network printer server and follow the instructions. The Add Printer Wizard walks you through the installation.

If you have printer driver software from the printer's manufacturer, you should use those drivers to set up your printer. When the Add Printer Wizard asks you to select the manufacturer and model of your printer, be sure to click the Have Disk . . . button to install those drivers.

Pausing a Document

You can pause a document that is in the queue to print. Pausing a document does not stop the printer. Other documents that are not paused continue to print.

To pause a document:

1. Click the Start button. The Start menu appears.

2. Point to Settings on the menu. The Settings menu appears.

3. Click Printers. The Printers folder appears.

4. Double-click the icon of the printer you want to pause or restart to open Print Manager.

5. Select the document that you want to pause.

6. From the Document menu, choose Pause.

Pausing the Printer

You can pause a printer to halt all printing. Keep in mind that when you pause a printer, the printer completes printing any information that has already been sent to the printer before printing completely pauses.

To pause or resume your printer:

1. Click the Start button. The Start menu appears.

2. Point to Settings on the menu.

3. Click Printers. The Printers folder appears.

4. Double-click the icon of the printer you want to pause or restart to open Print Manager.

5. Choose Printer⇨Pause Printing to pause the printer.

If a check mark appears next to the Pause Printing command, the printer is paused. To restart the printer, click the Pause Printing command again. The check mark disappears, and the printer resumes printing.

You can pause a printer only if the printer is attached to the computer you are using. For example, you cannot pause a network printer from your own computer. The Pause Printing command is unavailable if you have turned off spooling.

A quick way to pause the printer is to perform Steps 1–3. Then you right-click the printer whose properties you want to change and choose Pause Printing from the menu that appears.

Printing a File

To print an open document, choose File⇨Print.

To print a document that is not open, drag the document from My Computer or Windows NT Explorer to the Printer icon in the Printers folder. Windows NT launches to the appropriate application, issues the print command to that application, and then closes the application. The document prints automatically.

Printing a Font Sample

To print a font sample:

1. Click the Start button. The Start menu appears.

2. Point to Settings. The Settings menu appears.

3. Click Control Panel from the menu. The Control Panel appears.

4. Double-click the Fonts icon to open the Fonts folder.

5. Double-click the icon for the font you want to print. A sample page appears, showing the font and information about the font.

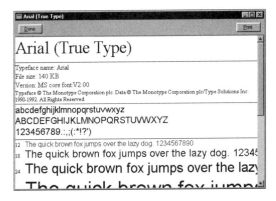

6. Click the Print button. The Print dialog box appears.

7. Click OK to print the document.

8. Click the Done button to close the sample font window.

To select more than one font, hold down the Ctrl key while clicking the fonts you want.

Restarting a Print Job

To restart a document:

1. Click the Start button. The Start menu appears.

2. Point to Settings on the menu. The Settings menu appears.

3. Click Printers. The Printers folder appears.

4. Double-click the printer that contains the document you want to restart.

5. Select the document to restart.

6. Choose Document⇨Restart to restart printing.

When you restart a document, that document prints again from the first page. If other, higher-priority documents are in the queue, however, they print first.

Resuming Printing

To resume printing a paused document:

1. Click the Start button. The Start menu appears.

2. Point to Settings on the menu. The Settings menu appears.

3. Click <u>P</u>rinters. The Printers folder opens.

4. Double-click the icon of the printer you want to pause or restart to open Print Manager.

5. Select the paused document that you want to continue printing.

6. Choose <u>D</u>ocument⇨<u>R</u>esume.

If you are printing to a network printer, you can pause only the documents that you have printed, unless you have been given full rights to control a printer.

Setting a Default Printer

To specify a default printer:

1. Click the Start button. The Start menu appears.

2. Point to <u>S</u>ettings on the menu. The Settings menu appears.

3. Click <u>P</u>rinters. The Printers folder opens.

4. Right-click the icon for the printer that you want to use as the default printer.

5. Choose Set As De<u>f</u>ault from the menu.

If a check mark appears next to the Set As De<u>f</u>ault command, the printer is set as the default printer.

Setting the default printer as the one you use the most is a good idea. Many Windows-based programs use the default printer automatically, unless you specify otherwise.

Sharing Your Printer

A quick way to open the Sharing dialog box is to perform Steps 1 through 3 in the preceding section and then right-click the printer whose properties you want to change. Choose S<u>h</u>aring from the menu that appears.

Stopping Printer Services

To stop all printing services on your computer:

1. Click the Start button. The Start menu appears.

2. Point to <u>S</u>ettings on the menu. The Settings menu appears.

3. Click Control Panel. The Control Panel window appears.

4. Double-click the Services icon. The Services dialog box opens.

5. Scroll through the list of services and select Spooler.

6. Click the Stop button. When asked, "Are you sure you want to stop the Spooler service?" click the Yes button.

To restart printing services, follow Steps 1 through 5 and then click the Start button.

Testing Your Printer

To print a test page to your printer:

1. Click the Start button. The Start menu appears.

2. Point to Settings on the menu. The Settings menu appears.

3. Click Printers. The Printers folder appears.

4. Right-click the icon for the printer to which you want to print a test page.

5. Choose Properties from the menu. The Properties dialog box opens.

6. From the General tab, click the Print Test Page button. A dialog box appears, asking whether the test page printed correctly.

Check to see whether the document printed correctly. If it did, click the Yes button. If it did not, click the No button. Windows NT displays a Help screen showing troubleshooting steps that you can take to fix the problem.

Viewing Document Properties

To view the properties of documents waiting to be printed:

1. Click the Start button. The Start menu appears.

2. Point to Settings on the menu. The Settings menu appears.

3. Click Printers. The Printers folder appears.

4. Double-click the printer icon. The print queue with all print jobs listed appears.

5. Select the document whose properties you want to view.

6. Choose Document⇨Properties. The document Properties dialog box appears.

From this dialog box, you can change the time that the document prints, change the priority of the document, or change the person who is notified when the document completes printing.

Select the Page Setup tab or the Advanced tab to view how the document will print. Note that you can make no changes from these tabs.

Viewing Documents Waiting to Print

To view documents waiting to be printed:

1. Click the Start button. The Start menu appears.

2. Point to Settings on the menu. The Settings menu appears.

3. Click Printers. The Printers folder opens.

4. Double-click the icon for the printer that you want to look at. The print queue appears, listing all print jobs.

Part VII

Reaching Out with Windows Messaging and Outlook Express

With Windows Messaging or Outlook Express, you can send, receive, and store electronic mail from one convenient place. And you can reach anyone, anytime, anywhere. All you need is an e-mail address. Microsoft Outlook Express is Microsoft's replacement for Windows Messaging. If you have the Full Installation of the Windows NT 4 Service Pack 4 or the Internet Explorer 4 CD-ROM, you have Outlook Express. Most people use Outlook Express for Internet e-mail, but you can also use it to access MS Mail, cc:Mail, CompuServe, America OnLine (AOL), and Microsoft Exchange Server (versions prior to Version 5).

In this part . . .

- ✔ **Creating and sending e-mail**
- ✔ **Organizing messages**
- ✔ **Printing messages**
- ✔ **Working with attachments**

About Windows Messaging and Outlook Express

When you open Windows Messaging or Outlook Express, you see the Viewer, which is your window to information. The left side of the Viewer displays sets of folders, and the right side displays the contents of the selected folder. From Windows Messaging or Outlook Express, you can send and receive mail, organize and manage information, and access and exchange information with other users.

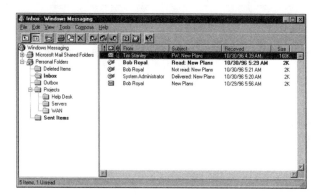

Adding an Attachment in Windows Messaging

In addition to text e-mail messages, Windows Messaging allows you to send binary files, such as word-processing files or spreadsheets.

To insert a file in a message that you are creating:

1. In the message, position the insertion point where you want to insert the file.

2. Choose Insert⇔File or click the Insert File button. The Insert File dialog box appears.

3. Using the Internet File dialog box, select the drive or folder that contains the file you want to insert from the Look in drop-down list box.

4. In the File name box, type the name of the file that you want to insert or select the file from the file list window.

5. Specify how you want to insert the file in the Insert as section:

   • Insert the file as text, select the Text only option button.

   • Insert the file as an application icon, select the An attachment option button. (This is the most common selection.)

   • Link the attachment, select the Link attachment to original file option button.

6. Click OK.

Adding an Attachment in Outlook Express

In addition to text e-mail messages, Outlook Express allows you to send binary files, such as word-processing files or spreadsheets.

To insert a file in a message that you are creating:

1. Choose Compose➪New Message, press Ctrl+N, or click the Compose Message button on the toolbar to open the New Message Window.

2. Choose Insert➪File Attachment or click the Insert File button on the toolbar. The Insert Attachment dialog box appears.

3. Using the Insert Attachment dialog box, select the drive or folder that contains the file you want to insert from the Look in drop-down list box.

4. In the File name box, type the name of the file that you want to insert or select the file from the file list window.

5. Click <u>A</u>ttach. The attachment shows up as an icon in the lower-left corner of the New Message window.

Addressing a Message in Windows Messaging

Before you can send a message, you must address it. To address an open message by using the Address Book:

1. Choose <u>T</u>ools⇨Address <u>B</u>ook or press Ctrl+Shift+B in the Windows Messaging message window. The Address Book dialog box appears.

2. To select a name from the address list, type the name or the first part of the name in the Type Name Or Select From List box. The list scrolls to match the letters you type.

3. To add a selected name to an address box, click the T<u>o</u> button or the <u>C</u>c button.

You also can insert a name in the T<u>o</u> box by double-clicking the selected name in the Address Book.

4. Click OK.

You also can address a message by typing the names of recipients directly in the To and Cc boxes in the New Message form. Separate multiple names with a semicolon (;). An even quicker way to enter a name is to type part of the name and click the Check Names button in the toolbar. If the text you type matches an entry in the address book, Windows Messaging automatically enters that name. If what you type matches multiple names, then the Address Book dialog box appears, displaying all names that match your entry. You can select the correct person from that dialog box.

Addressing a Message in Outlook Express

Before you can send a message, you must address it. The easiest way to do this, if you know the e-mail address, is simply to type the address in the To: text box. If you don't know the address of the person to whom you want to send the e-mail, but the person is listed in your Address Book, you can use the Address Book to select the address. To address an open message by using the Address Book:

1. Choose <u>T</u>ools⇨Select <u>R</u>ecipients or click the Select Recipients from a List button (looks like a Rolodex card) next to the word *To*. The Select Recipients dialog box appears.

2. To select a name from the list, type the name or the first part of the name in the Ty<u>p</u>e Name Or Select From List box. The list scrolls to match the letters you type.

3. To add a selected name to an address box, click the T<u>o</u> button, the <u>C</u>c (for Carbon Copy), or the <u>B</u>cc (for Blind Carbon Copy — the other recipients don't see who receives the Bcc) button.

You also can insert a name in the T<u>o</u> box by double-clicking the selected name.

4. Click OK. The selected names appear in the New Message window.

You also can address a message by typing the names of recipients directly in the To, Cc, and Bcc boxes in the New Message form. Separate multiple names with a semicolon (;).

An even quicker way to enter a name is to type part of the name and click the Check Names button in the toolbar. If the text you type matches an entry in the address book, Outlook Express automatically enters that name. If what you type matches multiple names, then the Check Names dialog box appears, displaying all names that match your entry. You can select the correct person from that dialog box.

Closing a Message

To close a message in either Windows Messaging or Outlook Express, use one of the following methods:

✦ Choose <u>F</u>ile⇨<u>C</u>lose.

✦ Click the message's Close box.

✦ Press Alt + F4

If you have entered anything in the message and try to close the message, you see a dialog box asking whether you want to save changes. If you click the <u>Y</u>es button, Windows Messaging saves the message in your Inbox. Outlook Express saves the message in your Drafts folder. You can open the saved message in the future, complete it, and then send the message. If you click the <u>N</u>o button, the message is discarded. If you click the Cancel button, you return to the message.

Copying a Message to a Folder in Windows Messaging

To copy an item to an existing folder:

1. If the message is not already open, select it. Then choose <u>F</u>ile⇨<u>C</u>opy. The Copy dialog box opens.

2. Click the plus sign next to the set of folders where you want to copy the item.

3. Select the folder to which you want to copy the item and then click OK.

You can create a new folder to copy the message to as you copy the message. To copy an item to a new folder, choose the New Folder button from the Copy dialog box, type a name in the Folder Name box, and then click OK.

You also can copy an unopened item by dragging it to the new folder while pressing Ctrl.

Copying a Message to a Folder in Outlook Express

To copy an item to an existing folder:

1. If the message is already open, choose File⇨Copy To Folder. The Copy dialog box opens. If the message is not open, right-click the message and choose Copy To from the pop-up menu.

2. Select the folder to which you want to copy the item. You may have to navigate to the desired folder by clicking the plus sign next to the name of the folder that contains the folder you are looking for.

3. Click OK. A copy of the message is magically transported to its new location. Note that the original message is not harmed.

You can create a new folder to copy the message to as you copy the message. To copy an item to a new folder, click the New Folder button in the Copy dialog box, type a name in the Folder Name box, and then click OK. The new folder appears as a subfolder of whichever folder was selected when you clicked the New Folder button.

You also can copy an unopened item by dragging it to the new folder while pressing Ctrl.

Deleting a Message in Windows Messaging

As your message base grows, so does the size of the Windows Messaging message file. So, pruning messages becomes an important part of housekeeping.

To delete an e-mail message, you can select an unopened message and then choose File⇨Delete. Or simply click the Delete button.

If the message is already open, you don't need to close it. Simply click the Delete button to delete the message.

To delete a list of sequential items, click the first item in the list, press and hold Shift, and then click the last item that you want to delete.

To delete a list of nonsequential items, click the first item in the list and press Ctrl as you click each item that you want to delete.

You can recover a message that you accidentally delete. Before exiting Windows Messaging, click on the Deleted Items folder, select the message that you want to recover, and drag that message back to the folder you deleted the message from.

Deleting a Message in Outlook Express

As your list of e-mail messages grows, so does the size of the Outlook Express message file. At some point, it's time to do some housekeeping.

To delete an e-mail message, you can select an unopened message and then choose Edit⇨Delete. Or simply click the Delete button.

If the message is already open, you don't need to close it. Simply click the Delete button to delete the message.

To delete a list of sequential items, click the first item in the list, press and hold Shift, and then click the last item that you want to delete.

When you delete a message, it doesn't really go away. Outlook Express moves the message to the Deleted Items folder. If you really want to get rid of a message click the Deleted Items folder, select the message you really, *really* want to delete, and then click the Delete button on the toolbar. If you would prefer to have Outlook Express empty your Deleted Items folder when you exit Outlook Express, follow these steps:

1. Select Tools⇨Options. The Options dialog box appears.

2. Click the General tab.

3. Click the Empty messages from the 'Deleted Items' folder on exit check box to place a check mark in it.

4. Click OK to close the Options dialog box.

The Options dialog box goes away. Now, each time you exit Outlook Express, the messages in your Deleted Items folder will be permanently deleted.

To delete a list of nonsequential items, click the first item in the list and press Ctrl as you click each item that you want to delete.

 You can recover a message that you accidentally delete. Click the Deleted Items folder, select the message that you want to recover, and drag that message back to the folder you deleted the message from.

Forwarding a Message in Windows Messaging

Perhaps you receive a message that needs more than just your eyes reviewing it. You can send that message to others.

To forward a message:

1. If the message is not already open, select it. Then click the Forward button on the toolbar.

2. In the To box, enter the addresses of the recipients.

3. To add comments or further instructions to the message, move the insertion point to the message body and type.

4. Click the Send button. If the message contains attachments, they are also forwarded.

 When you forward a private message (having set the Sensitivity to Private in the message properties dialog box), the message body in the original message is marked as protected or read-only. Recipients are unable to modify, cut, or copy the protected text.

Forwarding a Message in Outlook Express

Sometimes you receive messages that others need to see. Passing a message on to someone else is easy. To forward a message:

1. If the message is not already open, select it. Then choose Compose⇨Forward or click the Forward Message button on the toolbar. If the message is open, click the Forward button on the toolbar.

2. In the To box, enter the addresses of the recipients.

3. To add comments or further instructions to the message, move the insertion point to the message body and type.

4. Click the Send button. If the message contains attachments, they are also forwarded.

Moving Messages in Windows Messaging

Folders provide the basis for organizing information. You can organize the contents of any given folder by placing e-mail, text files, faxes, documents, meeting requests, and forms into folders. Perhaps you need to place related information in a single folder regardless of where it was created.

To move a message or other item to a folder:

1. If the item is not already open, select it. Then choose File⇨Mo_v_e. The Move dialog box appears.

2. Click the plus sign next to the set of folders where you want to move the item.

3. Select the folder to which you want to move the item.

4. Click OK.

To move a message or other item to an entirely new folder, follow Step 3 in the preceding steps, except you click the set of folders where you want to create the new folder (for example, click Personal Folders) and then click the New Folder button. Type the name of the new folder and then click OK.

To move a closed item, drag it to the new folder.

Moving Messages in Outlook Express

When you first start using Outlook Express, you may be content to keep all the message that you receive in your Inbox folder. Chances are, however, that as time goes on you will want to organize your messages by separating them into folders.

To move a message or other item to a folder:

1. If the item is open, choose File⇨_M_ove To Folder. The Move dialog box appears.

2. Click the plus sign next to the set of folders where you want to move the item.

3. Select the folder to which you want to move the item.

4. Click OK.

To move a message or other item to an entirely new folder, follow Step 3 in the preceding steps, except you click the set of folders where you want to create the new folder (for example, click Personal Folders) and then click the _N_ew Folder button. Type the name of the new folder and then click OK.

To move a closed item, drag it to the new folder.

Opening an Attachment in Windows Messaging

Attachments appear as icons embedded within the text of a message. To work with an attachment, you must open it.

To open an attachment, use one of the following methods:

+ Double-click the attachment icon.

+ Select the icon and then choose Edit➪File Object➪Open.

+ Right-click the icon and then choose Open.

Opening an Attachment in Outlook Express

To open an attachment in Outlook Express, use one of the following methods:

+ Double-click the attachment icon.

+ Right-click the icon and then choose Open.

Opening a Message in Windows Messaging

To open a message, use one of the following methods:

+ Double-click the message listed in the Inbox or another folder.

+ Select the message and then choose File➪Open.

+ Right-click the message and then choose Open.

Want to read through a list of messages? If you have a message open, you can open the next or previous item in the list by doing one of the following:

+ To open the next item in the list, choose View➪Next or click the Next button in the toolbar.

+ To open the previous item in the list, choose View➪Previous or click the Previous button in the toolbar.

Opening a Message in Outlook Express

To open a message, use one of the following methods:

+ Double-click the message listed in the Inbox or another folder.

+ Select the message and then choose File➪Open.

+ Right-click the message and then choose Open.

You can read through a list of messages. If you have a message open, you can open the next or previous item in the list by doing one of the following:

+ To open the next item in the list, choose View➪Next➪Next Message or click the Next button in the toolbar.

+ To open the previous item in the list, choose View➪Next➪ Previous Message or click the Previous button in the toolbar.

Printing an Attachment in Windows Messaging

To print attachments in a message:

1. Select or open the message with the attachment or attachments to print.

2. Choose File➪Print. The Print dialog box appears.

3. In the Options section of the Print dialog box, select Print Attachments and then click OK.

All attachments in the message print.

A quicker way to print an attachment is to open a message, right-click the attachment, and choose Print from the menu. Only that attachment prints.

Printing an Attachment in Outlook Express

To print attachments in a message:

1. Open the message with the attachment or attachments to print.

2. Right-click the attachment and select Print from the pop-up menu. The application used to create the attachment launches and immediately prints the document.

Printing a Message in Windows Messaging or Outlook Express

You can print any message that you send or receive.

Printing an open message

To print a message that you have open, choose File➪Print or click the printer icon. Clicking the printer icon causes the message to print immediately in its entirety. Choosing File➪Print brings up the Print dialog box, allowing you to print selected pages or multiple copies of the message.

Printing several messages

To print more than one message:

1. Select the folder containing the messages you want to print, or select the Inbox.

2. Select the first message to print and then, holding down the Shift key, select the last message to print. Or you can select the messages you want to print while pressing the Ctrl key.

3. Click the Printer icon to print all messages selected including attachments. Or choose File➪Print. When the Print dialog box opens, set the print options and click OK.

If you are using Windows Messaging, you can select the following options:

✦ **Start each item on a new page:** When marked, each message prints on its own page. When unmarked, messages are printed consecutively on a page.

✦ **Print attachments:** When marked, any attachment is printed. When unmarked, only the message prints.

If the items you want to print contain text and attachments, you can print only one selected file at a time. *See also* "Printing an Attachment," earlier in this part.

Quitting Windows Messaging

To quit Windows Messaging, choose File➪Exit.

To quit Windows Messaging and log off the current messaging session, choose File➪Exit and Log Off.

The Close command on the application Control menu closes only the active window. If no other Windows Messaging windows are open when you choose Close, you quit Windows Messaging.

Quitting Outlook Express

To quit Outlook Express, choose File⇨Exit or press Alt+F4.

The Close command on the application Control menu closes only the active window. If no other Outlook Express windows are open when you choose Close, you quit Outlook Express.

Replying to a Message in Windows Messaging

To reply to a message:

1. Select S or open the message you want to reply to and complete one of the following actions:

- To reply only to the sender, click the Reply To Sender button.

- To reply to the sender and everyone listed in the To and Cc boxes, click the Reply To All button.

2. Type your reply.

3. When you're finished typing, click the Send button.

Replying to a Message in Outlook Express

To reply to a message:

1. Open the message you want to reply to and complete one of the following actions:

- To reply only to the person who wrote the message, click the Reply To Author button.

- To reply to the person who wrote the message and everyone listed in the To and Cc boxes, click the Reply All button.

2. Type your reply.

3. When you're finished typing, click the Send button.

Retrieving a Deleted Message in Windows Messaging

To retrieve a deleted message or other item:

1. Click the Deleted Items folder.

2. Select the item that you want to retrieve and then choose File⇨Move.

3. Under Move this item to the selected folder, click the plus sign next to the set of folders where you want to move the item, select the folder to which you want to move the item, and then click OK.

To retrieve a deleted item, drag it from the Deleted Items folder to another folder.

Retrieving a Deleted Message in Outlook Express

To retrieve a deleted message or other item:

1. Click the Deleted Items folder.

2. Select the item that you want to retrieve and then choose Edit⇨Move To Folder.

3. Under Move the item(s) to the selected folder, click the plus sign next to the set of folders where you want to move the item, then select the folder to which you want to move the item.

4. Click OK.

To retrieve a deleted item, drag it from the Deleted Items folder to another folder.

If you selected Tools⇨Options, clicked the General tab, and placed a check mark in the Empty messages from the 'Deleted Items' folder on exit option, make sure that you recover any messages that you need from the Deleted Items folder before exiting Outlook Express.

Reviewing Sent Messages

By default, Windows Messaging and Outlook Express keep a copy of each message that you send in the Sent Items folder. To review messages in the Sent Items folder:

1. Open the Sent Items folder to see the list of sent messages.

2. Double-click the message you want to review. You can now read the message you sent.

Saving an Attachment in Windows Messaging

If you want to work with an attachment regularly or need to take the file to another, non-Windows, Messaging machine, you should save the attachment so that you can access it without using Windows Messaging.

To save an attachment contained in an open message:

1. If the message containing the attachment is open, choose File⇨Save As to display the Save As dialog box. If the message is not open, right-click the message in the list of messages and choose Save As from the menu.

2. Select the Save these Attachments only option button.

3. Choose a location in which to save the file from the Save in drop-down list box. You can save a message as a file in any directory on your computer.

4. Click Save.

Saving an Attachment in Outlook Express

To work with an attachment regularly or to take the file to another machine, you should save the attachment so that you can access it without using Outlook Express.

To save an attachment contained in an open message:

1. Open the message containing the attachment you want to save.

2. Right-click the attachment and select Save <u>A</u>s from the pop-up menu to display the Save Attachment As dialog box.

3. Choose a location in which to save the file from the Save in drop-down list box. You can save a message as a file in any folder on your computer.

4. Click <u>S</u>ave.

Saving a Copy of a Message in Windows Messaging

If you're a stickler for knowing who said what and when, you'll definitely want to keep copies of all your outgoing messages. By default, Windows Messaging saves a copy of every message you send in the Sent Items folder. If you (or some disk-space-hungry network admin type) have turned off this feature, never fear.

To save a copy of a message that you intend to send:

1. As you are composing a message, choose <u>F</u>ile⇔Proper<u>ti</u>es and then select the General tab.

2. Select the Save copy in Sent Items folder check box.

3. Click OK.

To save a copy of all messages you send:

1. Choose <u>T</u>ools⇔<u>O</u>ptions and then select the Send tab.

2. Select the Save a Copy of the Item in the 'Sent Items' folder check box and then click OK. Windows Messaging creates a Sent Items folder in which it saves a copy of a message when you send it.

Saving a Copy of a Message in Outlook Express

By default, Outlook Express saves a copy of every message you send in the Sent Items folder. If you have turned off this feature, you can still save a copy.

To save a copy of a message that you intend to send:

1. Type your e-mail address in the Cc box.

2. Send the message as you normally would.

To save a copy of all messages you send:

1. Choose Tools⇨Options and then select the Send tab.

2. Select the Save Copy of sent messages in the 'Sent Items' folder check box and then click OK. Outlook Express will once again save a copy of each message you send.

Saving an Incomplete Message in Windows Messaging

If you're interrupted while writing a message, you can save the work in progress to finish later.

To save an incomplete message, choose File⇨Save. Then close the message. The message is saved in your Inbox.

See also "Opening a Message in Windows Messaging," earlier in this part.

Saving an Incomplete Message in Outlook Express

To save an incomplete message, choose File⌐Save. Outlook Express displays a Saved Message dialog box informing you that the message was saved in your Drafts folder. Click OK to dismiss the dialog box, then close the yet to be completed message.

See also "Opening a Message in Outlook Express," earlier in this part.

Sending a Message with Windows Messaging

Sending a message with Windows Messaging involves three simple steps: addressing it, writing it, and sending it.

To send a message:

1. In Windows Messaging, choose Compose⇨New Message or click the New Message button.

2. To address the message, use one of the following methods:

- Click To or Cc to select names from the Address Book.

- In the To or Cc box, type the names of the primary recipients and users to whom you want to send a carbon copy. Separate multiple names with semicolons.

- If you want to send a message to one or more users as a blind carbon copy so that the original recipient cannot see that the message is being sent to others, choose Bcc Box from the View menu. Then click Bcc to select names from the Address Book or type the names of the users to whom you want to send a blind carbon copy in the Bcc box.

3. In the Subject box, type the subject of the message.

4. In the message body, type your message.

5. Choose File⇨Send or click the Send button.

You can assign different levels of importance to a message. With the message still open, click either the Importance: High button or the Importance: Low button. If the toolbar does not appear on your screen, choose View⇨Toolbar.

Sending a Message with Outlook Express

Sending a message with Outlook Express is as simple as A, B, C.

1. Click the Compose Message button on the toolbar.

2. Address the message. (*See also* the section on "Addressing a Message in Outlook Express," earlier in this part.)

3. In the Subject box, type the subject of the message.

4. In the message body, type your message.

5. Add attachments, if desired.

6. Choose File⇨Send Message or click the Send button.

You can assign different levels of importance to a message. With the message still open, select Tools⇨Set Priority and then choose High, Normal, or Low from the submenu that appears.

Sending or Deleting a Message at a Certain Time in Windows Messaging

With Windows Messaging, you can send a message at a certain time or have a message deleted from a recipient's Inbox after a specified time.

To set the time to send or delete a message that you are composing:

1. Choose File⇨Properties.

2. Click the Send Options button and select one or both of the following:

- To send a message later, choose Send This Item, select In, and then specify the number of minutes, hours, days, or weeks in which the message should be sent.

- To set a time for the message to be deleted, choose Expire This Item, select In, and then specify the number of minutes, hours, days, or weeks in which the message should be deleted.

3. Click OK.

Note that this option is available only if it is supported by the e-mail system used on your network.

Starting Windows Messaging

If you installed Windows Messaging when you installed Windows NT, Windows Messaging is already located on your desktop. It's the Inbox icon.

To start Windows Messaging, double-click the Windows Messaging icon on the desktop. If Windows Messaging starts automatically, you're ready to fire off e-mails.

If you get the Choose Profile dialog box when you double-click the Windows Messaging icon, follow these steps:

1. In the Profile Name list box, select the name of the profile you want to use or choose New to create a profile.

2. Choose Options to specify any of the following:

- To set the selected profile as the default, select the Set As Default Profile check box.

- To log on to each information service included in the selected profile each time you start Windows Messaging, select the Show Logon Screens For All Information Services check box.

3. Click OK.

Starting Outlook Express

If you're running Outlook Express for the first time, you'll find that it's easy to both set up and use. Outlook Express has built-in migration tools, so that if you've been using a different e-mail program, it's easy for you to access your existing e-mail messages and address book entries.

You can get going with Outlook Express in just a few simple steps.

1. Start Outlook Express in either of the following ways:

- Double-click the Outlook Express icon (with the envelope) on the desktop.

- Click the Start button, select Programs⇨Internet Explorer⇨ Outlook Express.

When you launch Outlook Express for the first time, the Internet Connection Wizard automatically appears and walks you through the Outlook Express setup process. The Wizard prompts you for your basic Internet access account information and clearly explains all setup options along the way.

2. Answer the questions the Wizard asks you. You will need to know your e-mail address, the names of your incoming and outgoing mail servers, your logon account name and password, and how you connect to the Internet (via a local area network or using a phone line). If you don't know the answers to these questions, you will need to check with your Internet Service Provider or your network administrator.

3. After you've provided this info, you are all set.

Part VIII

Using All Those Accessories

Included with Windows NT 4 is an array of accessories, utilities, and games. Many of these accessories are mirror images of applications found in Windows 95 and/or Windows 98, but some are unique to Windows NT 4.

In this part . . .

- ✔ Using Calculator
- ✔ Using Chat
- ✔ Playing CDs and videos
- ✔ Recording and playing back audio with Sound Recorder
- ✔ Storing information with Clipboard and ClipBook
- ✔ Playing games
- ✔ Using HyperTerminal
- ✔ Taking notes with Notepad
- ✔ Using Paint
- ✔ Connecting to another computer with Telnet
- ✔ Working with WordPad
- ✔ Character Map
- ✔ Volume Control
- ✔ Phone Dialer

About the Accessories

When you choose Programs⇨Accessories from the Start menu, you see a whole slew of programs hiding on the Accessories menu.

What It Is	Where It Is	What It Does
HyperTerminal	Start menu⇨ Programs⇨ Accessories⇨ HyperTerminal	A 32-bit communications application for modem communications (identical to the Windows 95 HyperTerminal application).
Wang Imaging for Windows NT	Start menu⇨ Programs⇨ Accessories	Excellent graphics viewer utility application with basic editing features (includes direct support for image acquisition from TWAIN-compliant scanners).
Phone Dialer	Start menu⇨ Programs⇨ Accessories	Utility that enables you to maintain a personal phone book and use a modem connected to your voice phone line to automatically dial phonebook entries.
CD Player	Start menu⇨ Programs⇨ Accessories⇨ Multimedia	Accessory that enables you to play music CDs in your system's CD-ROM drive.
3D Pinball	Start menu⇨ Programs⇨ Accessories⇨ Games⇨Windows NT CD-ROM	Cool 3-dimensional Pinball game, shows off the ActiveX capabilities of Windows NT 4. (*Warning:* Can be highly addictive!)
WordPad	Start menu⇨ Programs⇨ Accessories	A 32-bit editor that replaces the Write applications provided with earlier versions of Windows NT. WordPad utilizes common dialog boxes for opening, saving, and printing files, which makes entering long filenames easy. Although WordPad is not a full-blown word processor, it makes creating simple documents and memos easy for users.
Paint	Start menu⇨ Programs⇨ Accessories	A 32-bit graphics application that can read PCX and BMP files, and can write BMP files. Paint is an OLE server, enabling you to create OLE object information that can be embedded into or linked to other documents. Paint is also MAPI-enabled, so it is easily integrated with Microsoft Exchange for sending images in e-mail or fax messages.

What It Is	Where It Is	What It Does
Calculator	Start menu⇨ Programs⇨ Accessories	A mathematic and scientific calculator.
Character Map	Start menu⇨ Programs⇨ Accessories	A utility that enables you to view a complete character set for a font and copy characters to paste into a document. Enables you to quickly find special characters that don't appear on your keyboard.
Chat	Start menu⇨ Programs⇨ Accessories	A network communications tool that enables you to have a typed conversation with another user over the network.
Clipboard Viewer	Start menu⇨ Programs⇨ Accessories	A tool used to store common text or graphics that you or someone on the network is likely to use again and again. For example, a storage place for the company logo.
Clock	Start menu⇨ Programs⇨ Accessories	An accessory that displays the current time and date. Can display the time as a digital clock or an analog clock.
Notepad	Start menu⇨ Programs⇨ Accessories	An editor used for editing files or storing small amounts of information.
Telnet	Start menu⇨ Programs⇨ Accessories	A TCP/IP terminal tool that enables you to connect to other TCP/IP systems such as UNIX computers and some network devices such as bridges and routers.
Media Player	Start menu⇨ Programs⇨ Accessories⇨ Multimedia	Enables you to play sound or video files.
Sound Recorder	Start menu⇨ Programs⇨ Accessories⇨ Multimedia	Enables you to record and play back sound.
Minesweeper	Start menu⇨ Programs⇨ Accessories⇨ Games	A cool game of find the mines in the quickest time.
Freecell	Start menu⇨ Programs⇨ Accessories⇨ Games	Just like the card game.
Solitaire	Start menu⇨ Programs⇨ Accessories⇨Games	Just like the card game.

If you don't see one or all of these utilities on your system, you may not have installed them during Windows NT Setup. To install the utilities, double-click the Add/Remove Programs icon in the Control Panel, click the Windows NT Setup tab, and check the boxes for those items you want to install.

Calculator

Do you have numbers to crunch and you can't remember where you put your calculator? Windows NT offers several calculator functions built right in.

To start Calculator:

1. Click the Start button. The Start menu appears.

2. Point to Programs.

3. Point to Accessories.

4. Click Calculator to start the program.

To use your numeric keypad to enter numbers and operators, press the Num Lock key.

To perform a simple calculation:

1. Enter the first number in the calculation.

2. Click the + (plus sign) button to add, the – (minus sign) button to subtract, the * (asterisk sign) button to multiply, or the / (slash sign) button to divide.

3. Enter the next number in the calculation.

4. Enter any remaining operators and numbers.

5. Click the = (equal sign) button.

To perform a statistical calculation:

1. Choose View➪Scientific.

2. Enter the first piece of data.

3. Click the Sta button to display the Statistics Box and activate the Ave, Sum, s, and Dat buttons. Then click the Dat button.

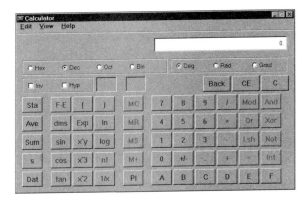

4. Enter the rest of the data, clicking Dat after each entry. The new data appears in the Statistics Box each time you click the Dat button.

5. Click the RET button in the Statistics Box to return to Calculator.

6. Click the button for the statistics function you want to use (Ave to calculate the mean of the values, Sum to sum the values, s to calculate standard deviation).

To perform a scientific calculation:

1. Choose View➪Scientific.

2. Click the option button corresponding to the number system you desire (decimal, hexadecimal, octal, or binary).

3. Enter the first number.

4. Click an operator.

5. Enter the next number in the calculation.

6. Enter any remaining operators and numbers.

7. Click the = (equal sign) button.

To convert a value to another number system:

1. Choose View⇨Scientific.

2. Enter the number.

3. Click the option button corresponding to the number system to which you want to convert (decimal, hexadecimal, octal, or binary).

CD Player

With CD Player, you can play an audio CD in the CD-ROM drive on your computer.

To start the CD Player:

1. Click the Start button. The Start menu appears.

2. Point to Programs. The Programs menu appears.

3. Point to Accessories. The Accessories menu appears.

4. Point to Multimedia.

5. Click CD Player.

CD Player looks very much like an actual CD Player with its play, stop, and pause buttons. CD Player also has buttons for advancing and moving back through a song or skipping tracks. The following table lists interesting options on the Options menu.

Character Map

You can use Windows NT Character Map to insert into your documents extended characters, happy faces, fancy Xs and Os, and other stuff you won't find on most keyboards.

To start the Character Map:

1. Click the Start button. The Start menu appears.

2. Point to Programs. The Programs menu appears.

3. Point to Accessories.

4. Click Character Map to start the program.

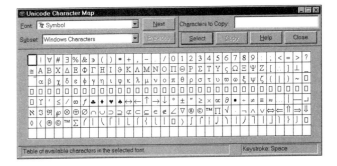

To insert a character into a document:

1. In the Unicode Character Map dialog box, click the arrow next to the <u>F</u>ont list box to view the drop-down list of available fonts.

2. Select a font. The character set changes to display the characters in the selected font.

3. Point to a character and then press and hold down the mouse button to see an enlarged picture of the character. You can also press the Tab key until the cursor is in the character selection area, and then use the arrow keys to see an enlarged picture of the character.

4. Double-click the character or click <u>S</u>elect. The selected character appears in the Ch<u>a</u>racters to Copy box.

5. Select as many characters as you want.

6. To place the characters showing in the Ch<u>a</u>racters to Copy box onto the Clipboard, click the <u>C</u>opy button.

7. Switch to the document into which you want to insert the characters.

8. Select the same font that you selected in the Unicode Character Map dialog box.

9. Position the cursor where you want the characters to appear.

10. Choose <u>E</u>dit⇔<u>P</u>aste.

TIP

When you paste into some programs, characters may lose the font you selected in the Unicode Character Map dialog box. To change the characters to the font you want, select them and format them for the font within the program.

Chat

Chat can be quite a handy tool. With Chat, you can connect to another computer on your network that is also using Chat and participate in a typed conversation. What you type is seen by the user that you are chatting with, and you can see what the other user types.

Starting Chat

To start Chat:

1. Click the Start button. The Start menu appears.

2. Point to Programs. The Programs menu appears.

3. Point to Accessories.

4. Click Chat.

The Chat window has two window panes. In the top pane, you see what you type. In the bottom pane, you see what the person you are chatting with types.

Starting a conversation

To start a conversation:

1. Start Chat.

2. Open the Conversation menu.

3. From the Conversation menu, click Dial. The Select Computer dialog box appears.

4. In the Select Computer dialog box, select the name of the computer you want to communicate with or type the name of the computer in the Computer text box.

5. Click OK. When the person on the other computer answers, you can begin chatting.

Answering a call

To answer a call:

1. Open Chat from the desktop. When someone calls you, Chat starts and appears as an icon on the desktop. Your computer starts beeping. If you have a sound card in your computer, Chat makes a sound like a phone ringing.

2. Start chatting.

Hanging up

To hang up from a chat, select <u>H</u>ang Up from the <u>C</u>onversation menu or click the Hang Up button.

Clipboard Viewer

The Clipboard temporarily stores information you are transferring between documents, and the ClipBook permanently stores information you want to save and share with others.

The Clipboard window shows the contents of the Clipboard. When you cut or copy information from an application, the information is placed onto the Clipboard and remains there until you clear the Clipboard or until you cut or copy another piece of information. You can paste the information into any document as often as you like.

Starting Clipboard Viewer

To start Clipboard Viewer:

1. Click the Start button. The Start menu appears.

2. Point to <u>P</u>rograms. The Programs menu appears.

3. Point to Accessories.

4. Click Clipboard Viewer to start the program.

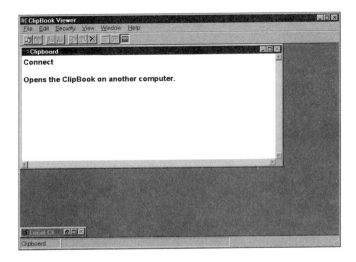

Because the Clipboard stores information in multiple formats, clearing it may free some memory to run an application.

Clearing the Clipboard

To clear the contents of the Clipboard:

1. Select the Clipboard icon or window.

2. On the toolbar, click the Delete button. You can also choose Edit⇨Delete.

Viewing the Clipboard's contents

To view the contents of the Clipboard, click the Clipboard icon in the ClipBook Viewer window.

Saving the Clipboard's contents

You can save the contents of the Clipboard either onto a page on the Local ClipBook or to a Clipboard file. The former is the preferred method because it is easier to view, retrieve, and share. Clipboard files cannot be shared.

To save the contents of the Clipboard on the Local ClipBook:

1. Select the Local ClipBook window.

2. Click the Paste button on the toolbar. You can also choose Edit⇨Paste.

3. In the Page Name box, type a name for the page that is to contain the information.

4. Click the Share Item Now check box to make this page available for others to use. If you click the Share Item Now check box, the Share ClipBook Page dialog box is displayed.

5. Make your selections and then click the OK button.

Games You Can Play

Windows NT doesn't just do work — it can play games, too.

To start a game:

1. Click the Start button. The Start menu appears.

2. Point to Programs. The Programs menu appears.

3. Point to Accessories.

4. Point to Games.

5. Click a game to start it.

HyperTerminal

You can use HyperTerminal and a modem to connect to a remote computer, even if it isn't running Windows. You can also use HyperTerminal to send and receive files or to connect to computer bulletin boards and other information programs.

Starting HyperTerminal

To start HyperTerminal:

1. Click the Start button. The Start menu appears.

2. Point to Programs. The Programs menu appears.

3. Point to Accessories.

4. Click HyperTerminal or one of the existing connections. The HyperTerminal Window opens.

Setting up a new connection

To set up a new connection:

1. Choose File⇨New Connection.

2. Type a name that describes the connection and click an appropriate icon. Then click the OK button.

3. Enter the information for the call and then click the OK button.

4. To dial the call, click the Dial button.

Calling a remote computer

To call a remote computer:

◆ Choose File⇨Open and then double-click the connection you want to use.

◆ Choose Call⇨Connect.

◆ Click the Dial button.

Sending a file to a remote computer

To send a file to a remote computer:

1. Make sure that the computer you're calling has the necessary file transfer to receive the file. Call the remote computer.

2. Choose Transfer⇨Send File. The Send File dialog box appears.

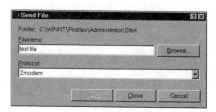

3. In the Filename box, type the path and name of the file. Or click the Browse button to display the Select File to Send dialog box.

To change the protocol you use to send the file, use the Protocol list box to select it.

4. To send the file, click the Send button.

You also can send a text file to the remote computer by choosing Transfer⇨Send Text File.

Receiving a file from a remote computer

To receive a file from a remote computer:

1. Call the remote computer. The software on the remote computer sends (downloads) the file to your computer.

2. Choose Transfer⇨Receive File. The Receive File dialog box appears.

3. Type the path of the folder in which you want to store the file. Or click the Browse button to display the Select a Folder dialog box.

4. In the Use receiving protocol list box, click the protocol the remote computer is using to send your file.

Changing port settings

To change the port settings for a particular modem connection:

1. Click the Start button. The Start menu appears.

2. Point to Programs. The Programs menu appears.

3. Point to Accessories.

4. Click the HyperTerminal that you want to change.

5. Choose File⇨Properties to display the Properties dialog box for that connection.

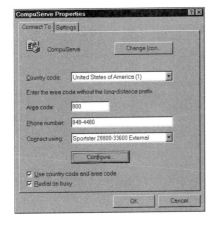

6. Click the Connect To tab.

7. Click the Configure button to display the Properties dialog box for that modem.

8. Click the Connection tab and then make the changes you need.

9. To change settings such as flow control and error correction, click the Ad*v*anced button and then make the changes you need.

Saving a HyperTerminal session

To save a HyperTerminal session to a file:

1. Choose <u>T</u>ransfer⇨<u>C</u>apture Text. The Capture Text dialog box appears.

2. Type a name that describes the file the text will be saved in.

3. Click the Start button.

To stop saving a HyperTerminal session to a file:

1. Choose <u>T</u>ransfer⇨<u>C</u>apture Text.

2. Click <u>P</u>ause or <u>S</u>top.

 You can also send the session text directly to a printer by choosing <u>T</u>ransfer⇨Capture to <u>P</u>rinter. When you end the call, the text is sent to your default printer.

Media Player

Media Player enables you to play different types of media files, such as music from a CD, audio from a sound file, or video from a video file.

The Media Player is intuitive to use because its buttons represent the buttons of a tape recorder.

Starting Media Player

To start Media Player:

1. Click the Start button. The Start menu appears.

2. Point to <u>P</u>rograms. The Programs menu appears.

3. Point to Accessories.

4. Point to Multimedia.

5. Click Media Player to start the program.

Opening and playing a media file

To open and play a file:

1. From Media Player, choose File⇨Open. The Open dialog box appears.

2. Use the Open dialog box to select the directory containing the media file and then select the file.

3. Click the Open button. The file loads into Media Player.

4. Click the Play button to play the Media file.

To stop playing the media file, click the Stop button.

Notepad

You can use Notepad to create or edit unformatted ASCII (text-only) files that are smaller than 64K.

Starting Notepad

To start Notepad:

1. Click the Start button. The Start menu appears.

2. Point to Programs. The Program menu appears.

3. Point to Accessories.

4. Click Notepad to start the program.

Keeping a log

To keep a log by using Notepad:

1. On the first line of a Notepad document, type **.LOG** at the left margin, making sure that you include the period.

2. Save the document.

Every time you open this file, Notepad appends the current time and date to the end of the file.

Paint

You can create, edit, or view pictures by using Paint. You can paste a Paint picture into another document you create or use it as your desktop background. You can even use Paint to view and edit scanned photos.

Starting Paint

To start Paint:

1. Click the Start button. The Start menu appears.

2. Point to Programs. The Programs menu appears.

3. Point to Accessories.

4. Click Paint to start the program.

Opening a file

To open a file:

1. Choose File⇨Open to display the Open dialog box.

2. In the Look in box, select the drive that contains the file you want to open.

3. Below the Look in box, select the folder that contains the file you want to open.

4. Select the file's name or type it in the File name box. Then click the Open button to display the file.

Using a picture as the desktop background

To cover the screen with repetitions of your bitmap, choose File⇨Set As Wallpaper (Tiled).

To put your bitmap in the center of your screen, choose File⇨Set As Wallpaper (Centered).

Note: You must save a picture before you can use it as wallpaper.

Printing a picture

To print a picture, choose File➪Print.

To see how the printed picture will look before you print, choose File➪Print Preview.

Setting margins and changing orientation

To set margins or change orientation, choose File➪Page Setup.

Phone Dialer

You can use Phone Dialer to place telephone calls from your computer by using a modem or another Windows telephony device. You can store a list of phone numbers you use frequently and dial the number quickly from your computer.

Dialing a number

To use Phone Dialer:

1. Click the Start button. The Start menu appears.

2. Point to Programs. The Programs menu appears.

3. Point to Accessories.

4. Click Phone Dialer to start the program.

5. Make sure that your modem and modem cables are connected correctly.

6. Type the number in dialable format or international format or click a number you've already dialed.

Calls in the dialable format are dialed exactly as they are shown, regardless of what location you specify. Calling cards cannot be used.

International format specifies the phone number in a format that can be dialed from any location or with a calling card.

7. Click Dial.

If you dial the same number frequently, you can store it on a speed-dial button.

Seeing a log of calls

To see a log of calls, choose Tools⇨Show Log. To dial a number in the log, double-click the log entry.

Selecting a calling card

To select a calling card to use:

1. Choose Tools⇨Dialing Properties.

2. Click the Dial using Calling Card check box.

3. Click the Change button to display the Change Calling Card dialog box.

4. Select a calling card with which you maintain an account from the Calling Card to use list box.

5. Click OK after selecting the Calling Card. The Dialing Properties dialog box reappears.

6. Click OK to save your changes.

Programming frequently used numbers

To store frequently dialed numbers:

1. Click an empty Speed-dial button to display the Program Speed Dial dialog box.

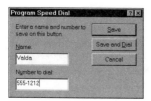

2. Fill in the requested information.

3. Click Save or Save and Dial.

Sound Recorder

Sound Recorder enables you to record and play back audio. You can, for example, record your voice, save the recording in a file, and give the file to someone else, who then can play back the file.

To use Sound Recorder, your computer must be equipped with a sound card, a microphone, and a pair of speakers.

Starting Sound Recorder

To start Sound Recorder:

1. Click the Start button. The Start menu appears.

2. Point to Programs. The Programs menu appears.

3. Point to Accessories.

4. Point to Multimedia.

5. Click Sound Recorder to start the program.

Opening and playing a sound file

To open and play a file:

1. From Sound Recorder, choose File⇨Open. The Open dialog box appears.

2. Use the Open dialog box to select the directory containing the sound file and then select the file.

3. Click the Open button. The file loads into Media Player.

4. Click the Play button to play the Media file.

Recording and saving a sound

To record and save a sound:

1. Start Sound Recorder. Ensure that your microphone is plugged in.

2. Click the Record button. You are now recording what the microphone picks up. When finished, click the Stop button.

3. Choose File⇨Save As. The Save As dialog box opens.

4. Select the directory in which to save the file and then type the name of the file in the File name text box.

5. Click Save.

Now that you have saved the sound, you can open it and play it back. You also can copy the sound file or e-mail it to someone else

Altering a sound file

You can do interesting things to the sound that you record with Sound Recorder. For example, you can mix the sound recording with another sound file, or you can add echo to a recording. The following table describes ways that you can alter a sound file.

Menu	Alteration	Description
Edit	Insert File	Enables you to insert another sound into the current sound file, combining the two files
Edit	Mix with File	Enables you to mix two sounds together so that you hear both at the same time when played
Effects	Increase Volume (by 25%)	Enables you to make a sound louder
Effects	Decrease Volume	Enables you to make a sound softer
Effects	Increase Speed (by 100%)	Makes a sound play twice as fast
Effects	Decrease Speed	Enables you to slow down a sound
Effects	Add Echo	Enables you to add an echoing affect to the sound
Effects	Reverse	Enables you to play a sound backwards

Before you start altering a sound, saving the original sound is a good idea. Saving in different files as you modify a sound file is also a good idea. By doing so, you can revert back to a modified version.

Telnet

The Telnet accessory is a terminal emulation program that lets you log on to a host (computer) running Telnet server software. With Telnet, you can control another computer from your Windows NT computer. The host may run UNIX, or NT, or another operating system.

Starting Telnet

To start Telnet:

1. Click the Start button. The Start menu appears.

2. Point to Programs. The Programs menu appears.

3. Point to Accessories.

4. Click Telnet to start the program.

The Telnet window appears on the screen.

Connecting to another computer with Telnet

To connect to another computer system using Telnet:

1. Start Telnet. The Telnet program appears.

2. Choose Connect⇨Remote System. The Connect dialog box appears.

3. Either type the name of the computer to connect to or select the name of a computer that you recently connected to from the Host Name drop-down list.

4. Click the Connect button.

When you successfully connect to a computer, you see information that that computer is displaying.

Disconnecting Telnet

After you are connected to another computer, you can disconnect from that computer. To do so, exit any program that you are running on the computer that you are connected to. Then choose Connect⇨Disconnect to hang up your connection.

Volume Control

If you have a sound card in your computer, you can use Volume Control to turn sound up or down from your computer's speakers, microphone, or CD-ROM drive.

Starting Volume Control

To start the Volume Control program:

1. Click the Start button. The Start menu appears.

2. Point to Programs. The Programs menu appears.

3. Point to Accessories on the Programs menu.

4. Point to Multimedia on the Accessories menu.

5. Click Volume Control to start the program.

Adjusting playback volume

To adjust the playback volume, drag the Volume Control slider up to raise the volume and down to lower the volume. To change the balance between the left and right speakers, drag the Balance slider.

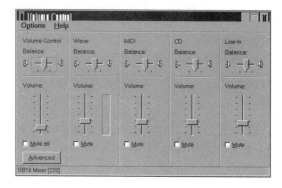

If your computer has more than one device (for example, a MIDI or Wave device), you can set the volume for each device.

To turn off the sound, click the Mute All check box in the Volume Control dialog box.

Adjusting recording volume

To adjust the recording volume:

1. Choose Options⇨Properties to display the Properties dialog box.

2. Click the Recording radio button.

3. Make sure that the device you want to adjust the volume for is checked and then click the OK button.

4. Drag the Volume Control slider up to raise the volume and down to lower the volume.

Adjusting voice-input volume

To adjust the voice-input volume:

1. Choose Options⇨Properties and then click the Other option button in the Properties dialog box.

2. Select Voice Commands from the drop-down list box.

3. Make sure that the device for which you want to adjust the volume is checked and then click the OK button.

4. Drag the Volume Control slider up to raise the volume and down to lower the volume.

To change the balance between the left and right speakers, drag the Balance slider.

WordPad

WordPad is a word processor for short documents. You can format documents in WordPad with various font and paragraph styles. Because WordPad comes with Windows NT, it's ideal for use as a word processor on your notebook computer.

Starting WordPad

To start WordPad:

1. Click the Start button. The Start menu appears.

2. Point to Programs. The Programs menu appears.

3. Point to Accessories on the Programs menu.

4. Click WordPad to start the program.

Creating a new document

To create a new document:

1. Choose File⇨New to display the New dialog box.

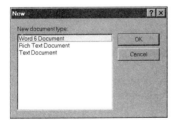

2. Click the file type you want to create and click OK. Then begin typing. You can choose Word 6, Rich Text, or Text Document formats.

To name a new file, choose File⇨Save As.

Saving changes

To save changes to a document, choose File⇨Save.

To save an existing document with a new name, click File⇨Save As and then type a new name in the File name box.

Opening a document

To open a document:

1. Choose File⇨Open to display the Open dialog box.

2. In the Look in list box, select the drive that contains the document you want to open.

3. Below the Look in box, select the folder that contains the document you want to open.

4. Select the document's name or type it in the File name box.

5. Click the Open button.

If you don't see what you're looking for, select a different file type from the Files of type list.

To open a document you opened recently, select its name from the bottom of the File menu.

Undoing an action

To undo your last action, choose Edit⇨Undo.

To undo a deletion, choose Edit⇨Undo.

Deleting text

To delete text:

1. Select the text you want to delete.

2. To remove text so that you can place it in another part of the document, choose Edit⇨Cut. To remove text entirely from the document, press the Delete key.

Selecting text

To select all the text in a document, choose Edit⇨Select All.

To cancel a selection, click anywhere in the document.

Searching for text

To search for text:

1. In the document, click where you want to start searching.

2. Choose Edit⇨Find to display the Find dialog box.

3. Enter the search text in the Find what box.

4. To find additional instances of the same text, click the Find Next button.

Inserting date and time

To insert the current date and time:

1. Click where you want the date and time to appear.

2. Choose Insert⇨Date and Time to display the Date and Time dialog box.

3. Select the format you want for the date or the time.

Changing text wrap

Can't see all your text? To change the way text wraps on your screen:

1. Choose View⇨Options to display the Options dialog box.

2. In the Word wrap box, select the wrapping option you want and then click OK.

After you turn on a Word wrap option, what you see is not what you get when you print the document. The Word wrapping options affect only how text appears on your screen. The printed document reflects the margin settings specified in the Page Setup dialog box.

Inserting bullets

Do you need to emphasize a point? Use bullets.

To create a bulleted list:

1. Click where you want the bullet list to start.

2. Choose Format⇨Bullet Style and then enter text. When you press Enter, another bullet is displayed on the next line.

3. To end the bullet list, choose Format⇨Bullet Style again.

Changing fonts

If you want to add flare, change the font.

To change a font type, style, and size:

1. Select the text you want to format.

2. Choose Format⇨Font.

3. Select the options you want and then click OK.

You can specify the font for new text by changing the font settings before you begin to type. To change the font for an entire document, choose Edit⇨Select All before choosing the Font from the Format menu.

Previewing your document

Do you want a preview of how your document will look after you print it?

To see how the document will look in print:

1. Choose File⇨Print Preview.

2. To return to the previous view from Print Preview, click the Close button.

Part IX

Maintaining Your Computer

The key to successfully managing and maintaining your system is knowing how to make changes to the system's various settings and configurations. In Windows NT 4, you make these changes using several different Windows NT utilities or tools found in the Control Panel.

In this part . . .

- ✔ **Making things more accessible**
- ✔ **Adding and removing programs**
- ✔ **Setting the screen display**
- ✔ **Modifying keyboard and mouse settings**
- ✔ **Getting mail**
- ✔ **Changing multimedia settings**
- ✔ **Understanding the network**

Accessibility Options

Windows 95 introduced special accessibility features for people with disabilities or special physical-access needs. The features include:

◆ Large screen fonts and high-contrast color schemes for individuals with visual impairments

◆ On-screen visual indication when sounds are made

◆ Special keyboard modifications that enable people with restricted movement to use the keyboard as a mouse, enter Ctrl, Shift, or Alt-based key sequences one key at a time (StickyKeys), direct Windows to ignore accidental keystrokes (FilterKeys), and make an audible sound when pressing the Caps Lock, Num Lock, and Scroll Lock keys (ToggleKeys)

To modify or view the Windows NT accessibility features by using the keyboard:

1. Press Alt+S to open the Start menu.

2. Press S to open the Settings menu.

3. Press C to open the Control Panel.

4. Use the arrow keys to select Accessibility Options and press Enter. The Accessibility Properties dialog box appears.

To modify or view the Windows NT accessibility features by using the mouse:

1. Click the Start button. The Start menu opens.

2. Point to Settings on the Start menu. The Settings menu appears.

3. Click Control Panel. The Control Panel window appears.

4. Double-click the Accessibility Options icon in the Control Panel.

The Accessibility Properties dialog box appears.

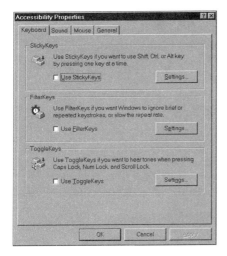

The Accessibility Properties dialog box contains four tabs. Each tab enables you to customize a specific part of Windows NT. The following table describes the tabs and the options that you can modify.

Click This Tab	To Make These Changes
Keyboard tab	Sets the StickyKeys, FilterKeys, and ToggleKeys options on or off, controlling the way Windows NT processes keystrokes
Sound tab	Provides visual notification when sounds are played
Mouse tab	Enables the keyboard's numeric keypad to act as a mouse
General tab	Controls configuration options related to Accessibility options, such as having accessibility features turn off automatically after a specified time period (useful if the PC is shared by multiple users) and providing audible notification when features are turned on or off

You can make changes to the Accessibility options by using the mouse or the keyboard, but using the mouse is easier. Simply click the tab you want to view, click a check box to select an option, and click a button to make a change to the option.

Adding and Removing Programs

The Add/Remove Programs icon enables you to do two things:

- ✦ Selectively install and remove Windows NT components, such as accessory programs, the Exchange client, wallpaper files, and screen savers.

♦ Install and remove applications, including all files that have been copied to your hard disk for that application, no matter what directory the files were copied to.

To open the Add/Remove Programs icon:

1. Click the Start button. The Start menu appears.

2. Point to Settings on the Start menu. The Settings menu appears.

3. Click Control Panel. The Control Panel window appears.

4. Double-click the Add/Remove Programs icon in the Control Panel. The Add/Remove Programs Properties dialog box appears

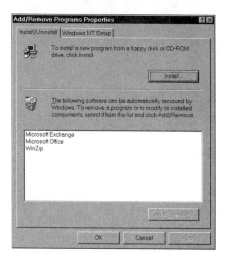

Adding and removing Windows NT components

To use the Windows NT Setup portion of the dialog box:

1. Open the Add/Remove Programs Properties dialog box.

2. Click the Windows NT Setup tab. A list of all the categories of Windows NT components and features displays. Components with check boxes containing a check are installed, and those components with unchecked boxes are not. Components with gray checked boxes are partially installed (at least one component).

- To see the individual components within a category, double-click the category name.

- To install a component that is not yet installed, select the check box next to it in the list.

- To remove a component from Windows NT, uncheck the box next to it in the list.

3. After you finish checking and unchecking boxes, click the OK button.

Windows NT installs or uninstalls the components you selected, and the program prompts you to insert the Windows NT 4 Installation CD, if necessary.

Installing programs

Generally, programs that you purchase come with their own installation program that you start from either disk 1 of the disk set or from the installation CD. However, another way to install a program is to use the Add/Remove Programs Properties:

1. Open the Add/Remove Programs Properties dialog box, as described in the preceding section.

2. Insert the diskette or CD containing the program to install.

3. Click the Install button in the Install/Uninstall tab. The Install Program From Floppy Disk or CD-ROM dialog box appears.

4. Click the Next button. Windows NT searches your disk drives and your CD-ROM drive for a program to install. Then it displays the Run Installation Program dialog box with the name of the program's installation program. If Windows NT does not find a program to install, it still displays the Run Installation Program dialog box, but you must type the name of the installation program manually or click the Browse button to find the program to install.

5. If the name of the installation program is correct, click the Finish button to begin installation. Optionally, you can click the Back button to return to the Install Program From Floppy Disk or CD-ROM dialog box.

When the installation program begins, follow the steps to install your program. When installation is complete, Windows NT returns you to the Control Panel.

Uninstalling programs

When you install a program, files are copied to the directory that you install the program to, but some of the program's files are often copied to other directories that you may not be aware of. Simply deleting the directory that the program resides in does not mean that you have completely deleted all the files originally copied to your hard disk. When you install a program, however, Windows NT tracks all files that are copied to your hard disk.

Using Uninstall to remove a program ensures that all files originally copied to your hard disk are removed.

To uninstall a program:

1. Open the Add/Remove Programs Properties dialog box as described in the previous set of steps.

2. In the box on the Install/Uninstall tab, click the program in the list of programs to uninstall.

3. Click the Add/<u>R</u>emove button.

4. Follow the steps displayed on-screen to uninstall the program that you selected. When complete, you will return to the Add/Remove Programs Properties dialog box.

5. Click OK when you are finished removing programs.

Note: Removing programs only removes the program files; it does not remove any of the data files that you may have created with the program you removed.

Date/Time

As its name implies, the Date/Time icon offers settings for the date and time, as well as the time zone for your Windows NT system.

To open the Date/Time icon:

1. Click the Start button. The Start menu appears.

2. Point to <u>S</u>ettings on the Start menu. The Settings menu appears.

3. Click <u>C</u>ontrol Panel. The Control Panel window appears.

4. Double-click the Date/Time icon in the Control Panel. The Date/Time Properties dialog box appears.

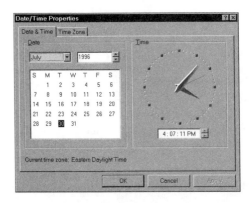

The following table describes the tabs available in the Date/Time Properties dialog box.

Click This Tab	To Make These Changes
Date & Time	Enables you to change the month, day and year, and the time of day.
Time Zone	Displays a map of the world from which you can click your location or select the time zone that you are in. Enables you to automatically adjust your computer's clock for daylight savings time.

Devices

Windows NT provides support for hardware devices (and some software services as well) using *device drivers*. These device drivers are copied to your Windows NT installation and configured by Windows NT when you install the hardware or software using the Control Panel icons, such as Network or SCSI Adapters. Although the management of these device drivers is largely automatic, you may need to examine or modify the Windows NT device drivers, such as starting and stopping them, to trouble-shoot a problem.

You can use the Devices icon of the Control Panel to view the list of installed Windows NT device drivers.

To open the Devices dialog box:

1. Click the Start button. The Start menu appears.

2. Point to Settings on the Start menu. The Settings menu appears.

3. Click Control Panel. The Control Panel window appears.

4. Double-click the Devices icon in the Control Panel. The Devices dialog box appears.

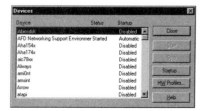

To the right of each listed device is the device's current status (for example, Started, if the driver is loaded, or blank, if the device is not loaded), and the *startup state* of the device. The startup state relates to how Windows NT loads the driver and what priority loading of the device is given.

The Sta<u>r</u>tup button on the right side of the dialog box controls the startup state of the device driver currently selected in the list. The possible startup types for device drivers in Windows NT are shown in the following table.

Type	What Happens
<u>B</u>oot	The highest priority startup type, boot-type device drivers are critical to the system's ability to boot and are loaded when the system starts.
<u>S</u>ystem	Devices with this startup type are critical to system operation and are loaded at system startup, after Boot devices.
<u>A</u>utomatic	Devices with this startup type are loaded automatically at system startup, after Boot and Startup devices.
<u>M</u>anual	These devices are not loaded when the system boots but may be loaded manually by either the user or a dependent device driver.
<u>D</u>isabled	These devices are not loaded at all. In addition, these drivers cannot be started manually by the user, although Windows NT can start them, if necessary. An example of a device in a Disabled startup state is a SCSI driver for a SCSI adapter that was removed from the system.

Changing the startup state of a Boot or Startup device driver can cause your Windows NT installation to stop booting properly. Be very careful when making changes to these types of devices.

Another feature of the Devices icon, which is new to Windows NT 4, is the ability to control which devices are loaded in different hardware profiles.

To enable or disable a device driver in a particular hardware configuration:

1. Select the device driver and click the H<u>W</u> Profiles button. A dialog box containing a list of all current hardware profiles displays, showing the status of the current device driver in each profile (enabled or disabled).

2. Select the profile and then click the <u>E</u>nable button to enable the device for that configuration or click the <u>D</u>isable button to disable the device for that configuration.

3. Click OK when you are finished.

For more information on creating a Hardware Profile, *see also* the "System" section later in this chapter.

Dial-Up Monitor

Windows NT provides a Dial-Up Networking feature that allows you to access remote computers or networks by using dial-up connections (for example, using an analog modem or ISDN terminal adapter). To monitor your Windows NT Dial-Up Networking sessions, you can use the Dial-Up Monitor icon in the Control Panel.

To open the Dial-Up Networking Monitor dialog box:

1. Click the Start button. The Start menu appears.

2. Point to Settings on the Start menu. The Settings menu appears.

3. Click Control Panel. The Control Panel window appears.

4. Double-click the Dial-Up Monitor icon in the Control Panel. The Dial-Up Networking Monitor dialog box appears.

The Dial-Up Monitor dialog box contains three tabs, as described in the following table.

Use This Tab	To Make This Change
Status	This screen shows statistics about the current Dial-Up Networking session, such as connection speed, total number of incoming and outgoing bytes and frames, and information on any transmission errors (useful in troubleshooting problems). You can select the device you want to monitor by using the Device drop-down list box.
Summary	The summary screen displays the networks and users currently connected through Dial-Up Networking, and the devices used to make the connections. Windows NT 4 supports multiple simultaneous Dial-Up Networking sessions on a single Windows NT system and displays all connections in the summary window. From this tab, you can display details of a line or hang up a line.

(continued)

Use This Tab	To Make This Change
Preferences	The Preferences screen enables you to set various options for monitoring Dial-Up Networking sessions. These options include the ability to play sounds when certain events occur in the Dial-Up Networking session, include the Dial-Up Monitor in the Windows NT task list, and display on-screen status lights similar to those found on external modems.

Display

The Control Panel's Display icon is used to set display-related settings in Windows NT. These settings include such items as screen resolution, colors, wallpaper, screen saver, and monitor type.

To open the Display icon:

1. Click the Start button. The Start menu appears.

2. Point to Settings on the Start menu. The Settings menu appears.

3. Click Control Panel. The Control Panel window appears.

4. Double-click the Display icon in the Control Panel. The Display Properties dialog box appears.

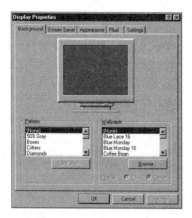

The Display Properties dialog box has five tabs that enable you to change different aspects of the screen. For example, you can change the background, set up a screen saver, or select the type of video adapter you have in the computer. The following table describes each tab, as well as the options you can find on each tab.

Click This Tab	To Change These Settings
Background tab	Enables you to set a background pattern and desktop wallpaper. The options in this tab are similar to the options found in the Desktop icon of the Windows 3.x Control Panel.
Screen Saver tab	Offers a screen saver that appears after a specified time period of inactivity (mouse and keyboard).
Appearance tab	Controls various aspects of the Windows NT desktop, such as the fonts and colors used for various types of windows. You also can select from a list of predefined desktop schemes that automatically set a number of these options. You can create your own custom schemes and then save and name them by clicking the Save As button.
Plus! tab	Gets its name from the Plus! Pack introduced in Windows 95. The Windows 95 Plus! Pack is an optional add-on containing a variety of new desktop schemes, utilities, and screen savers. In Windows NT, several of the Windows 95 Plus! Pack features are incorporated into the base product. Those options, such as stretching the wallpaper to fit the entire screen and *full drag* (showing a window and its contents while it's being dragged across the screen) are located here.
Settings tab	Sets important information about the Windows NT video display, including screen resolution, number of displayable colors, font size for screen characters, and video refresh rate. Change the Windows NT video driver by clicking the Display Type button. Most changes to the video display require that you test the new configuration using the Test button before Windows NT accepts the changes. Windows NT informs you of this requirement if you attempt to exit the dialog box by clicking the OK button prior to testing the new settings.

Fonts

The Fonts icon of the Control Panel enables you to manage fonts in your Windows NT system. You can view those fonts that are currently installed and either add or remove fonts from the system.

To open the Fonts icon:

1. Click the Start button. The Start menu appears.

2. Point to Settings on the Start menu. The Settings menu appears.

3. Click Control Panel. The Control Panel window appears.

4. Double-click the Fonts icon in the Control Panel. The Font window opens, displaying all fonts currently installed in Windows NT.

By default, the Fonts folder displays in large icon format all the screen and TrueType fonts installed on your Windows NT system. TrueType fonts are denoted with a TT inside the icon; all other fonts contain an A inside the icon. The View menu contains choices that enable you to change the font list display. For example, if you want Windows NT to display the icons in a list with additional information such as the font filename, you can choose View⇨List. If you want to view fonts in terms of their similarity to another font, choose View⇨List Fonts by Similarity.

Also, many fonts come in sets of four: the main (normal) font and three variations of the main font (italic, bold, and bold italicized). Other fonts may offer only a normal and bold version or only the regular font with no variations. If you want Windows NT to display only the main fonts and not the variations, choose View⇨Hide Variations (bold, italic, and so on).

To add a new font to your computer:

1. Choose File⇨Install New Font to open the Add Fonts dialog box.

2. Select the drive and folder that contain the fonts you want to add from the Fol_ders and the Dri_ves drop-down lists.

3. Select the fonts that you want to add from the List of _fonts list box and then click the OK button.

To select more than one font to add, press and hold down the Ctrl key and then click the fonts you want.

To select a range of fonts in the list, press and hold down the Shift key while dragging the mouse pointer over the fonts.

To add fonts from a network drive without using disk space on your computer, make sure that the _Copy fonts to Fonts folder check box is not checked.

To delete a font from your computer:

1. Open the fonts folder.

2. Click the icon for the font you want to delete.

3. Choose _File⇨_Delete or press the Delete key.

Internet

The Internet icon in the Control Panel enables your Window NT system to use a proxy server to access the Internet.

To open the Internet icon:

1. Click the Start button. The Start menu opens.

2. Point to _Settings on the Start menu. The Settings menu appears.

3. Click _Control Panel. The Control Panel window appears.

4. Double-click the Internet icon in the Control Panel. The Internet Properties dialog box appears.

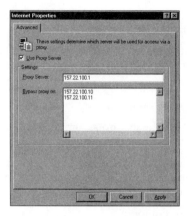

The Internet Properties dialog box enables you to set whether the machine uses a proxy server and what the IP address (or host name) of the proxy server is. Enter the server name or IP address, a colon and the port to use in the Proxy Server field. For example, if the proxy server's name is *main proxy* and the port that is used for the proxy is 8080, you type the following:

    main_proxy:8080

In addition, the Bypass proxy on field is provided for entering the host names or IP addresses of any internal servers that can be accessed from the machine by using TCP/IP. Internal TCP/IP-based servers are considered part of what is called an *intranet,* or private TCP/IP-based network, and normally do not require the use of a proxy server. Only Internet (outside) servers are accessed by using the proxy server.

Keyboard

To modify keyboard-related settings in your Windows NT system, you can use the Keyboard icon in the Control Panel.

To open the Keyboard icon:

1. Click the Start button. The Start menu appears.

2. Point to Settings on the Start menu. The Settings menu appears.

3. Click Control Panel. The Control Panel window appears.

4. Double-click the Keyboard Icon in the Control Panel. The Keyboard Properties dialog box appears.

The Keyboard Properties dialog box contains three tabs that enable you to change the response of the keyboard, the language layout of the keyboard, and the type of keyboard. The following table describes the contents of each tab.

Click This Tab	*To Change This Setting*
Speed tab	You can adjust speed-related keyboard settings in this tab. Repeat delay enables you to adjust the time before a character begins repeating, and Repeat rate lets you control how quickly characters are repeated. You also can adjust the cursor blink rate in this tab. Use the Click here and hold down a key to test repeat rate text box to test changes that you make.
Input Locales tab	In this tab, you can specify which international keyboard layout(s) load when Windows NT starts. Multiple locales may be installed and switched between by using a hot key (or set by selecting one of the layouts on this screen).
General tab	In this tab, you can define the keyboard driver used by Windows NT for your keyboard. (In earlier versions of Windows, changing the keyboard required using Windows Setup.) Click the Change button to open a window and select your keyboard type. If your keyboard ships with a special Windows NT-specific driver to enable support, you also can click the Have Disk button to load the driver from a vendor-supplied driver disk.

Mail

The Control Panel Mail icon is used for configuring the Windows
NT Messaging Client. The Messaging Client is a universal client
inbox that receives messages from different information services.

 To open the Mail icon:

1. Click the Start button. The Start menu appears.

2. Point to Settings on the Start menu. The Settings menu
appears.

3. Click Control Panel. The Control Panel window appears.

4. Double-click the Mail icon in the Control Panel. The Windows
Messaging Settings Properties dialog box appears.

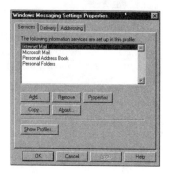

To add or remove Windows Messaging services or to make
changes to those you have already configured, click the Services
tab in the Windows Messaging Settings Properties dialog box.

To add a service, click the Add button and select a new service
from the provided list. To remove a service, select the service
name and click the Remove button.

To make changes to an installed Windows Messaging service,
select the service name and click the Properties button.

The Internet Mail service (and most other Windows Messaging
services) also provides additional tabs for important information
about the service. Examples of this information include such
options as:

♦ Whether the service's server is directly accessible by using a
local area network or requires a Dial-Up Networking session
(and which Dial-Up Networking session is used).

+ Whether remote (offline) mail options are used for this service. Remote mail enables you to view and edit messages and folders offline when not connected to a service (for example, using a laptop computer when traveling).

Profiles is another feature of the Windows Messaging client that you can select in the Services tab. With Profiles, you can create custom Windows Messaging profiles for each user. You also can set Windows Messaging to give you a choice of profiles when it is started or automatically select a particular profile every time. To manage Windows Messaging profiles, click the Show Profiles button at the bottom of the Service tab window. The Mail dialog box appears, displaying a list of all existing profiles.

Each profile may use one or more of the available Windows Messaging services. The most common use of Profiles is to create a different profile for every user of the system. This process provides each user with a personal profile with which to access personal messages. Also, multiple profiles for the same user may be created using different sets of services (for example, a second profile for the same user can be created to use only the Internet Mail service). Profiles may be added and removed using the Add and Remove buttons, and copies of existing profiles may be made using the Copy button.

To specify where incoming messages are delivered, and in what priority order outgoing mail is processed, click the Delivery tab. After you are finished adding, removing, or changing profiles, click the Close button.

Incoming messages can be stored in either of two locations: a network server-based mailbox, named Mailbox Username (for networked users only), or inside of a personal folder file stored on the local system. This location may be set by clicking entries in the list of choices next to the Deliver new mail to the following location portion of the Delivery tab window. To set the priority order in which outgoing messages from information services are processed, select the service name and use the up- and down-arrow keys on the right to move services up or down in the list.

To configure options for using Windows Messaging Address Books, click the Addressing tab. Windows Messaging Address Books are lists containing mail addresses from which you may select when creating new messages. Generally, you have only two different address books, although you can have more. The first type of address book is your Personal Address Book, where you store the addresses you create and use. The second type of address book is one that is provided to you if you are connected to an electronic mail system.

In the Addressing tab, you can select which address book you
want to display first when you select an address. You also can
select which address book you want to use to store personal
addresses. If more than one person uses this Windows NT system,
you can indicate which personal address book is *your* personal
address book. You can add address books by clicking the Add
button and delete books by clicking the Remove button.

Microsoft Mail Postoffice

The Microsoft Mail Postoffice icon in the Windows NT Control
Panel enables you to create and manage a Microsoft Mail
Workgroup Postoffice, which may be located on your machine or
any other machine on your network.

To open the Microsoft Mail Postoffice icon:

1. Click the Start button. The Start menu appears.

2. Point to Settings on the Start menu. The Settings menu appears.

3. Click Control Panel. The Control Panel window appears.

4. Double-click the Microsoft Mail Postoffice icon in the Control
Panel. The Microsoft Workgroup Postoffice Admin dialog box
appears.

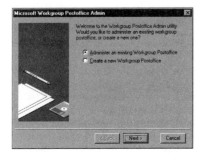

After you launch Microsoft Mail Postoffice by double-clicking its icon, you have two options: Create a new Workgroup Postoffice or administer an existing one. After selecting the desired option and clicking Next, you're asked to supply the location of the Workgroup Postoffice to create or manage.

If you are creating a new Postoffice for your workgroup, you need to supply a folder name for the new Postoffice. (Optionally, you can click the Browse button to use the mouse to locate the folder, much as you use Explorer to locate files.) Under most circumstances, you want to supply the root folder of one of your hard disks for the name, such as C:\ or D:\. When Windows NT offers to create the new Postoffice, it automatically names the folder wgpo0000.

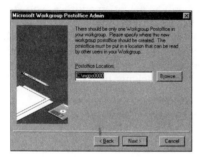

Because you are creating a new Postoffice, you also must enter the account information of the mail administrator. Here, you enter the name of the administrator, such as Administrator; the mailbox name, such as Admin; the password (use something besides the default PASSWORD); and information about how to contact the Administrator of the postoffice. If you are the administrator, don't use your own name; use the name *Administrator*. After you are done, click OK.

Finally, in order for your new Postoffice to be accessible by other workgroup users, you need to share the Postoffice folder and give other network users with accounts in the Postoffice full access permissions (read, write, and delete).

If you choose to administer an existing workgroup postoffice and have selected the location of the postoffice to administer, you are asked to enter the mailbox name and password of the administrator. Note that this is the mailbox name, and not the full name, of the administrator (Admin, for example).

Administrating a postoffice means that you can add users by clicking the Add Users button, change users by clicking the Details button, or remove users by clicking the Remove button. Click the Shared Folders buttons to view information about mail folders that postoffice users have created. When you are finished administering the postoffice, click the Close button.

Modems

You can use the Modems icon in the Control Panel to configure your modem (and accompanying Unimodem driver) in Windows NT. The first time you use the icon, Windows NT offers to automatically detect your modem. You also have the option of choosing the modem manually from a list (by checking the appropriate box in the window before clicking the Next button).

To open the Modems icon:

1. Click the Start button. The Start menu appears.

2. Point to Settings on the Start menu. The Settings menu appears.

3. Click Control Panel. The Control Panel window appears.

4. Double-click the Modems icon in the Control Panel. The Modems Properties dialog box appears.

Your installed modem appears in the Modems Properties dialog box. In this dialog box, you can add or remove modems and configure the properties for modems already installed.

To configure a modem already installed, select the modem and click the Properties button. Two tabs are available. General enables you to change modem properties, such as the speaker volume and communications rate. The other tab, Connection, enables you to change some of the intricacies of your communications port connection. For example, you can change the Data bits, Parity, and Stop bits, which are three important settings for modem communications. You also can indicate the following:

+ The modem should wait for a dial tone before beginning dialing.

+ A call should be canceled if a connection is not made within a number of seconds that you specify.

+ A call should be disconnected if no information is being transferred for a number of minutes specified by you.

If you click the Advanced button, you can set up the modem for error control, flow control, and modulation type, and you can enter any extra settings that you desire. Generally, you should always leave the advanced settings at their defaults, unless you are told otherwise by someone familiar with modem communications.

A final option in the Modems Properties dialog box is the Dialing Properties. To specify how your calls are dialed, click the Dialing Properties button. The Dialing Properties dialog box appears.

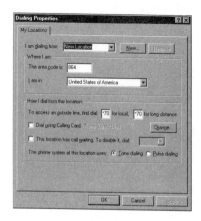

The purpose of the Dialing Properties dialog box is to specify how your modem should dial the phone when placing outgoing calls. For example, if the line from which you are dialing has call waiting, you may want to disable call waiting by checking the appropriate box and choosing the call waiting disable string from the supplied list. (For many areas, the string *70 is used to disable call waiting for just one call.)

If this computer will be used from more than one area (for example, a laptop computer), you also should use the I am dialing from drop-down list to define properties for each of the locations. Each location you define can have an entirely different set of dialing properties (different area codes, long-distance prefixes, and so on). Click the New button to define new locations.

Mouse

The Control Panel's Mouse icon enables you to configure various properties of your mouse or other pointing devices, such as trackballs and pen mice.

To access the Mouse Properties dialog box:

1. Click the Start button. The Start menu appears.

2. Point to Settings on the Start menu. The Settings menu appears.

3. Click Control Panel. The Control Panel window appears.

4. Double-click the Mouse icon in the Control Panel. The Mouse Properties dialog box appears.

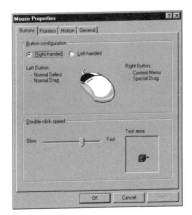

The Mouse Properties dialog box contains four tabs from which you can alter the way that the mouse works. The following table describes those tabs, as well as what you can find on each tab.

Click This Tab	*To Change These Options*
Buttons tab	In the Buttons tab, you can set several different options, such as whether the mouse is right-hand or left-hand oriented. You also can set the mouse's double-click speed in this tab (by dragging a sliding bar that goes from slow to fast), and you can test the speed by double-clicking the text box in the lower-right corner of the dialog box. A successful double-click makes a jack-in-the-box appear or disappear. The faster the double-click speed setting, the faster you need to double-click the mouse's primary button to make Windows NT register the action as a double-click.
Pointers tab	The Pointers (called cursors in previous versions of Windows NT) tab controls the types of pointers used in Windows NT. Different pointers appear in Windows NT depending on what object or section of the screen the pointer is currently over. NT supports both animated and non-animated pointers. You can select pointer schemes by clicking the Scheme drop-down list box, or you can select custom pointers for individual pointer types by highlighting the name of the pointer's function, clicking the Browse button, and selecting a pointer to be used for that pointer type. You also can create your own schemes by making all desired pointer customizations and clicking the Save As button.
Motion tab	The Motion tab controls two mouse properties: the speed at which the mouse pointer moves across the screen (by dragging the Pointer speed sliding bar in the Mouse Properties dialog box) and whether the pointer should always jump to the default button in any dialog box (set by checking a check box). The latter feature, Snap mouse to the default button in dialogs, makes quickly selecting default options in dialog boxes easy.
General tab	As with the Keyboard Properties dialog box General tab, the Mouse Properties icon General tab is the new location of the Mouse configuration portion of Windows NT Setup in previous versions of Windows NT. This tab enables you to select which type of mouse you are using in Windows NT, which in turn sets the driver Windows NT uses for the mouse.

Multimedia

The Multimedia icon is used to configure all aspects of the multimedia features of your Windows NT system.

To make changes to Multimedia devices:

1. Click the Start button. The Start menu appears.

2. Point to Settings on the Start menu. The Settings menu appears.

3. Click Control Panel. The Control Panel window appears.

4. Double-click the Multimedia icon in the Control Panel. The Multimedia Properties dialog box appears.

The Multimedia Properties dialog box enables you to change settings for your sound card, MIDI devices, video devices, and CD-ROM. This dialog box has five different tabs for making changes. The following table describes these tabs.

Click This Tab	*To Do This*
Audio tab	Sets various audio-related options, such as output and recording volume, preferred audio input/output devices, and whether or not the volume control icon is displayed. Turning this last option on enables you to click an icon to access the Windows NT volume control utility.
Video tab	Offers video-playback options in Windows NT. By default, Windows NT supports playback in the AVI (Audio Video Interleave) format using Microsoft Video for Windows. Among the options available for video playback are full-screen or windowed playback of videos (the windowed option offers a variety of choices for the size of the playback window) and the Advanced button, which tells Windows NT to use 16-bit code rather than 32-bit code for video playback. This setting provides maximum compatibility for 16-bit video applications, but it should be used only if you are experiencing problems with video playback.

(continued)

Click This Tab	To Do This
MIDI tab	Offers MIDI-related options for Windows NT. You can specify which MIDI instrument should be used for MIDI playback, customize MIDI output configurations, and add new MIDI instrument definitions by clicking the Add <u>N</u>ew Instrument button.
CD Music tab	Sets audio options for your CD-ROM drive(s). In the top drop-down list box, select which CD-ROM to configure. The <u>H</u>eadphone option controls the audio output level for devices connected to the CD-ROM drive's headphone jack (usually located on the front of the drive).
Devices tab	Displays a list of all installed multimedia drivers in Windows NT. You can add, remove, and configure multimedia drivers. The Multimedia Drivers is an Explorerlike tree, with categories for each type of multimedia device. To view the installed devices of that type, double-click the category name to expand the tree. To set the properties of a particular multimedia device, select the device and click the <u>P</u>roperties button.

Network

The Network icon is the key to one of the most important (and complex) Windows NT features: its advanced networking capabilities. Windows NT provides an enormous array of network-related features, virtually all of which are set by first double-clicking the Network icon.

To make changes to your network settings:

1. Click the Start button. The Start menu appears.

2. Point to <u>S</u>ettings on the Start menu. The Settings menu appears.

3. Click <u>C</u>ontrol Panel. The Control Panel window appears.

4. Double-click the Network icon in the Control Panel. The Network dialog box appears.

When you open the Network dialog box, you see five tabs with options on each tab. These tabs are Identification, Services, Protocols, Adapters, and Bindings. The following table describes each tab.

Use This Tab	To Do This
Identification	Identifies both the Windows NT computer's network name and the name of the workgroup or domain to which the computer belongs. You also are prompted for this information the first time you set up any networking components on your Windows NT system.
Services	Enables you to add and remove different network services. Network services give you the ability to share files with others, connect to other computers by viewing computer names, perform simple network management (SNMP), and many other things.
Protocols	Displays the current network protocols that are installed, such as TCP/IP, NetBEUI, and IPX/SPX, and enables you to install or modify network protocols. *Protocols* are like grammar in that each computer has to follow certain rules when "talking" to other computers on a network.
Adapters	Enables you to add, remove, or change network adapters in your computer system.
Bindings	Shows connections that are made between network services, network adapters, and network protocols. With bindings, you can change the order that Windows NT makes these connections and even disable connections that you have made. Generally speaking, you should not make changes to bindings.

Three primary components make up Windows NT networking (in lowest to highest order): adapters, protocols, and services. A fourth component, bindings, is a collection of settings that define the various relationships between these other three network components. The fifth component, identification, enables you to change the name of the computer, as well as the workgroup or domain to which it is connected. The next few sections provide information about each of these components.

The three primary network components

Services (more specifically, network services) are the highest-level networking component of Windows NT. Services are Windows NT software components that enable your Windows NT system to communicate with different systems. Services communicate with other computers using protocols (sometimes referred to as *transport protocols*), and protocols, in turn, exchange information over the network adapters installed in your system. In order for your Windows NT system to work properly on your network, you must have the correct adapters, protocols, and services installed. The following paragraphs give a more in-depth explanation of adapters, protocols, and services.

Adapters are the hardware devices (such as network adapter cards, ISDN terminal adapters, or modems configured for Dial-Up Networking) that physically connect your computer to a network. For your Windows NT computer to participate in a network, it must have one or more network adapters installed (or the Remote Access Service). The Adapter tab in the Network dialog box lists the adapters currently installed on your computer.

Protocols, in human language, are a set of standards or procedures used by more than one party to communicate and cooperate. Computer protocols are very similar: They are the languages computers speak (using adapters) over a network to communicate with one another. Computers must have at least one protocol in common to communicate over a network.

Windows NT is capable of speaking more than one protocol over the same network adapter. If a protocol is loaded and configured for use with a particular network adapter, the protocol is said to be *bound* to that adapter. To configure protocols in Windows NT, you click the Protocols tab in the Network dialog box.

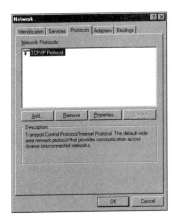

Different protocols are available in Windows NT, but only a few are used for most networking applications. For a protocol to be useful for file- and print-sharing in Windows NT, it must support the Server Message Block (SMB) protocol, the core protocol used by all Windows NT, Windows 95, Windows for Workgroups, and Microsoft LAN Manager servers. Currently, three such protocols are available in Windows NT: NetBEUI, NWLink IPX/SPX, and Microsoft TCP/IP. The other protocols are provided for specialized connections with other types of computers and network environments.

Services are high-level software components that enable Windows NT to perform networking tasks. Windows NT services use the adapters and network protocols installed on one system to communicate with other systems on the network. When networking is installed in Windows NT, a default set of services is automatically installed, including the ability to act as both a server (share files and printers) and a workstation (share the files and printers on other servers). Depending on your network configuration, you also may need to install additional services on your Windows NT 4 system.

Services

The Services tab of the Network dialog box shows you the installed network services, and you can add or remove services
from the network configuration. The following table describes the
services that are available with Windows NT.

Use This Service	To Do This
Server	Enables a Windows NT system to share files and printers with other computers on the network.
Workstation	Connects a Windows NT computer to the shared files and printers on other computers across a network (this service is also known as the Windows NT redirector).
Remote Access Service	Enables a Windows NT computer to use Dial-Up Networking to access remote network servers, including Windows NT Remote Access Servers (RAS) and servers such as those used by Internet Service Providers for Internet access.
Computer Browser	Creates and maintains a list of computers currently available on the network, enabling you to graphically browse available servers across the network (for example, when connecting shared resources).
NetBIOS Interface	Stands for Network Basic Input/Output System. NetBIOS is a networking application program interface (API) that provides service allowing applications to communicate across a network. This networking service should not be confused with NetBEUI, which is a network transport protocol (although NetBEUI does use and require NetBIOS to function).

Use This Service	To Do This
Remote Procedure Call (RPC) Configuration	Enables your Windows NT system to participate in the Remote Procedure Call Client/Server system used by applications. Basically, RPC enables your computer to carry on specific conversations with other computers to carry out necessary tasks.
Simple TCP/IP Services	A set of TCP/IP connectivity utilities, including PING, FTP (client), TFTP, FINGER, and other popular TCP/IP-based utilities.
FTP Server	FTP is the File Transfer Protocol. The FTP Server Service (previously included only with the NT Server product) enables your Windows NT system to act as an FTP server to systems running FTP client software.
Microsoft Peer Web Services	Enables a Windows NT 4 system to serve as a personal HyperText Markup Language (HTML)-compliant Web server for internal or external (Internet) network access.
Microsoft TCP/IP Printing	Enables Windows NT to print to and manage TCP/IP-based printers on a network.
SNMP Service	Enables Windows NT to work with SNMP (Simple Network Management Protocol) software so that a network manager can monitor various aspects of a system.
Client Service for NetWare	Enables your Windows NT system to log onto and use shared devices on a Novell NetWare server.
Network Monitor Agent	Passes network communication information to monitoring programs so that network managers can "tune" a network to work more efficiently.

To install a new service, click the Services tab and then click the Add button and select the desired service from the list provided. To remove a service, select the service to remove and then click the Remove button. To configure a service already installed, select the service name and click the Properties button. Note that many services are not configurable with the Properties dialog box and will produce an error message if this is done.

Protocols

The Protocols tab lists the protocols that are currently installed on the Windows NT computer. Windows NT supports quite a number of protocols. The following table lists the protocols available with Windows NT and describes the purpose of the protocols.

Use This Protocol	To Do This
AppleTalk Protocol	Enables Macintosh computers to share files and printers attached to the Windows NT computer.
DLC Protocol	The Data Link Control protocol that is most commonly used to communicate with Hewlett-Packard network printers.
NetBEUI Protocol	A protocol that is used for small networks. This is the protocol that was most common with Windows for Workgroups.
NWLink IPX/SPX Compatible Transport	This is the protocol used by Novell NetWare servers. Use this protocol if you are communicating with other NetWare servers.
Point To Point Tunneling Protocol	This is a secure protocol that enables a Windows NT computer to communicate securely over the Internet with a corporate network.
Streams Environment	An environment that enables some compatible UNIX network drivers to be moved to the Windows NT environment.
TCP/IP Protocol	The popular protocol that is used to connect to the Internet. This protocol was made popular in the UNIX operating system and has proven to be a very good protocol for large and small networks.

To add a protocol to Windows NT:

1. Click the Protocols tab, then click the Add button and select the protocol to add.

2. Click OK. Windows NT generally needs to copy the protocol files to your computer. A dialog box instructs you to indicate where the necessary files can be found. Type the location of the files and then click Continue.

To remove a protocol, select the protocol to remove from the Network Protocols window and then click the Remove button.

To change the settings of the protocol, select the protocol and click the Properties button. Use the Update button to update a protocol.

For some changes that you make, you must restart Windows NT for those changes to take effect. Windows NT displays a message if you must restart your computer.

Be careful when you remove or change a protocol. This action could render your computer inoperable on the network.

Adapters

You can use many types of network adapters with Windows NT. Before you purchase a network adapter, check the Windows NT Hardware Compatibility List (HCL) to ensure that the adapter you are interested in is compatible with Windows NT.

To add a network adapter:

1. From the Network dialog box, click the Adapters tab.

2. Click the Add button.

3. From the Network Adapters dialog box, select the adapter that you are installing and then click OK.

4. Windows NT asks you to indicate where it can find the files necessary for the adapter. Type the location and then click Continue.

To remove a network adapter, select the adapter that you desire to remove and then click Remove. Remember, as long as you do not physically take the network adapter out of your computer, you can add back the network adapter software.

To make changes to the network adapter, select the adapter and click the Properties button. Make the necessary changes and then click OK.

To update the files for your network adapter, select the network adapter in the box and click the Update button.

Remember, most changes that you make in the Adapters tab require that you restart your computer. Windows NT prompts you with a message if you must restart the computer.

Identification

To change the computer's name and/or workgroup or domain name, click the Identification tab and then click the Change button to bring up the Identification Changes dialog box.

To change the computer name, type the name (up to 15 characters long) in the Computer Name box. The name cannot be the same as another computer in the domain or workgroup and cannot be the same name as the domain or workgroup itself.

Bindings

The Bindings tab makes available for view all the current bindings between all currently installed network adapters, network services, and protocols. You can also enable and disable individual bindings on a case-by-case basis. To make a change to the Bindings, open the Network dialog box and click the Bindings tab.

In the Show Bindings for drop-down list box, select whether to show bindings for all services, all protocols, or all adapters. The Bindings list box looks much like the Windows NT Explorer. Select a binding to change and then click the Enable button to enable a binding, the Disable button to disable a binding, or the Move Up and Move Down buttons to change the order that a binding binds.

Do not disable a network binding unless you are sure of the result. Certain networking functions in Windows NT may cease to function properly. The rule to follow is "If in doubt, leave it enabled."

PC Card (PCMCIA)

For users of laptops and other systems with PC Card (also called PCMCIA) devices, the Control Panel PC Card (PCMCIA) icon provides support for these devices.

To make changes to your PC Card settings:

1. Click the Start button. The Start menu appears.

2. Point to Settings on the Start menu. The Settings menu appears.

3. Click Control Panel. The Control Panel window appears.

4. Double-click the PC Card icon in the Control Panel. The PC Card (PCMCIA) Properties dialog box appears.

Windows NT does not support the *hot swapping* of PC Card/PCMCIA devices (that is, changing the device while the system in turned on). Windows NT loads devices for all hardware at startup and requires that any PC Card/PCMCIA device that is used during a session be installed at the time the system is started. Changing PC Card devices while the system is on causes unpredictable results.

Ports

The Ports icon enables you to configure your serial communications (or COM) ports in Windows NT.

To make changes to your Ports settings:

1. Click the Start button. The Start menu appears.

2. Point to Settings on the Start menu. The Settings menu appears.

3. Click Control Panel. The Control Panel window appears.

4. Double-click the Ports icon in the Control Panel. The Ports dialog box appears.

The Ports dialog box displays all COM ports that are currently available for configuration in Windows NT. This list was created when Windows NT was first installed on your system.

Don't be alarmed if one of your ports is missing from this list; the lost port is probably the port to which your pointing device (mouse or trackball) is connected. Windows NT intentionally removes this port from the Ports dialog box and instead configures that serial port as a system device called PointerPort0. Not listing the port prevents the port settings for the device from being incorrectly or inadvertently modified, which could cause the pointing device to stop functioning properly.

If subsequent communication ports are added to the system later, you should add those ports manually by clicking the Add button because Windows NT does not automatically detect and configure them. When adding a port, knowing several key pieces of information (which you will be asked to supply) about the new port is important:

◆ COM Port number

◆ Base I/O Port Address

◆ Interrupt Request Line (also called the IRQ or hardware interrupt)

◆ FIFO Enabled — Whether the UART (Universal Asynchronous Receiver/Transmitter) chip driving the port contains a First-In, First-Out (FIFO) buffer

To delete a port, select the port and click the Delete button. To configure a port's settings, select the port and click the Settings button. The Settings dialog box appears.

The Settings dialog box offers settings for the COM port, such as baud rate, data bits, stop bits, parity, and flow control. For each item that you set in the Settings dialog box, check for the correct settings in the documentation that comes with the device you are attaching to the port. If no mention of COM port settings is made, try leaving the settings at the default. If the default settings do not work, experiment with different settings or contact the device's manufacturer for help with configuring the port.

The Advanced button in the Settings dialog box allows you to configure low-level information about the COM port — the same information asked when using the Add button to add a new port. This information includes the COM Port number, Base I/O Port Address, Interrupt Request Line (IRQ), and whether a FIFO buffer is present on the port.

Regional Settings

The Regional Settings Control Panel icon enables you to control how country-specific information (such as time, date, and currency) is displayed.

To make changes to the Regional Settings:

1. Click the Start button. The Start menu appears.

2. Point to Settings on the Start menu. The Settings menu appears.

3. Click Control Panel. The Control Panel window appears.

4. Double-click the Regional Settings icon in the Control Panel. The Regional Settings Properties dialog box appears.

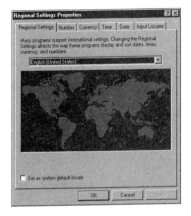

The Regional Settings Properties dialog box contains six different tabs that enable you to change settings for your region. You can also display information based on the peculiarities of another region.

SCSI Adapters

SCSI (Small Computer Systems Interface) is a broadly supported specification for hardware peripherals that has many advantages, especially in the Windows NT environment.

Most SCSI adapters normally allow up to seven intelligent peripherals, either internal or external, to be attached in a daisy-chain fashion to the SCSI host adapter. Some adapters allow for more devices. (These adapters are also called SCSI host adapters because they are the host for SCSI devices.) The SCSI interface is used by a wide variety of peripheral devices, including hard disks, CD-ROM and optical drives, floppy drives, scanners, tape drives, and a range of other devices. SCSI specifications have evolved over the years, including Narrow SCSI (SCSI-1), Fast SCSI (SCSI-2), Wide SCSI, Fast/Wide SCSI (SCSI-3), and Ultra SCSI. Each specification carries its own set of rules, data transfer rates, and device capabilities. However, all are capable of being used under Windows NT, as long as a native Windows NT 4 device driver for the host adapter exists.

The SCSI specification also allows for devices to operate simultaneously and independently of one another and the host system's CPU. This arrangement translates to better overall system performance. Due to its multitasking and low CPU usage features, SCSI is the preferred mass storage system for Windows NT computers. Windows NT was designed with SCSI in mind, and SCSI's advantages are fully exploited.

To make changes to your SCSI Adapters settings:

1. Click the Start button. The Start menu appears.

2. Point to Settings on the Start menu. The Settings menu appears.

3. Click Control Panel. The Control Panel window appears.

4. Double-click the SCSI Adapters icon in the Control Panel. The SCSI Adapters dialog box appears.

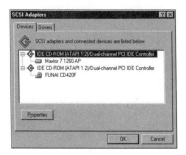

The SCSI Adapters dialog box has two tabs, Devices and Drivers. The Devices tab displays a list of all currently installed SCSI Adapters, including IDE adapters, and their attached peripherals. When a + appears next to an adapter name in the window, you can double-click the adapter name to expand the tree and view the devices attached to that adapter. Or you can just click the plus symbol of the option to expand.

You also may click the Properties button in this tab to view the properties of the currently selected SCSI adapter. This action opens a dialog box for the adapter that you selected, which in turn contains several tabs displaying information about the adapter name, manufacturer, Windows NT driver used for the adapter, and resource settings used by the adapter. Examples of those settings are the Interrupt Request Line (IRQ), Input/Output base address, and Upper Memory addresses.

You can add and remove SCSI adapter drivers in Windows NT in the Drivers tab. To add a SCSI adapter to your Windows NT configuration:

1. Install and configure the new SCSI host adapter in your system using the manufacturer's installation instructions provided with the adapter.

2. Boot Windows NT.

3. Double-click the SCSI Adapters icon in the Control Panel.

4. Click the Drivers tab and click the <u>A</u>dd button.

5. Select from the list of SCSI adapter manufacturers and models provided. If your adapter is not listed, but you have a disk containing a Windows NT 4 driver for the adapter, select the <u>H</u>ave Disk option and install the driver from the manufacturer-supplied disk.

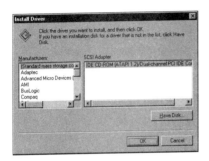

6. After Windows NT finishes installing the driver, you need to shut down and restart your system in order for the adapter support to take effect.

Every SCSI adapter you install has a corresponding Windows NT device driver that is automatically installed and configured when the device is added to the system. This driver is added to the list of drivers appearing in the Control Panel Devices icon and configured with a startup type of Boot (the highest priority). This high-priority status ensures that the driver is among the first loaded so that Windows NT can boot properly.

To remove a SCSI adapter from your Windows NT installation, select the adapter in the list and click the <u>R</u>emove button. Windows NT asks you to confirm the removal of the device.

Server

Windows NT has peer-networking capabilities, meaning that it may act as both a network client and a server to other network users. To manage features and view statistics related to the server aspects of your Windows NT computer, you can use the Control Panel's Server icon.

To make changes to your Server settings:

1. Click the Start button. The Start menu appears.

2. Point to <u>S</u>ettings on the Start menu. The Settings menu appears.

3. Click Control Panel. The Control Panel window appears.

4. Double-click the Server icon in the Control Panel. The Server dialog box appears.

The Server dialog box shows several statistics related to current server resources and usages. The following table describes these statistics.

Statistic	What It Does
Sessions	Shows the total number of users currently having remote connections to this computer.
Open Files	Displays the number of files currently open (being accessed) by connected users on this computer.
File Locks	Displays the total number of *file locks* in use by users remotely connected to this computer. A file is locked when someone is making changes to a file, and no other users should be allowed to make a change to that file.
Open Named Pipes	Displays the total number of open *named pipes* on this computer. A named pipe is a process that enables one computer to communicate with another computer.
Description	Enables you to enter a description for a Windows NT computer, which is displayed in dialog boxes and other places generated by network clients browsing available network servers.

A variety of buttons appear at the bottom of the Server dialog box. These buttons enable you to view and control details about the computer's resources. Each button controls a different function and opens a different dialog box, enabling you to display statistics about the function and make changes to that function. The following table lists each button that you can click in the Server dialog box and a description of the button's purpose.

Click This	To Do This
Users	Clicking this button brings up the User Sessions dialog box, which shows the users currently connected to your Windows NT computer and what shared resources are currently being accessed by those users. You also can disconnect a user or all users from your computer in this dialog box.
Shares	This button is similar to the Users button, but it gives a share-centric view of open resources rather than the user-centric one shown by the Users button. Clicking the Shares button displays the Shared Resources dialog box. As with the User Sessions dialog box, you can use the Shared Resources dialog box to disconnect one or all users that are connected to your computer.
In Use	Clicking this button displays the Open Resources dialog box, which lists all the currently open resources on your Windows NT computer, along with information on which user is accessing the resource, what type of access is active for the resource, the total number of file locks on the resource, and the pathname of the resource (for example, the full pathname of an open file). From the Open Resources dialog box, you can close a single resource that someone is using or close all resources being used.
Replication	Windows NT can be configured to automatically duplicate a specific set of folders between Windows NT computers across the network. This feature is known as *replication*, and it has many potential uses for Network Administrators. Windows NT Workstation can be configured to import directories from a Windows NT Server. Windows NT Workstation cannot be set up to replicate its own directories.
Alerts	Enables you to specify names of computers or users that should receive a message when certain events happen to your computer. For example, you can indicate a few users that should be notified when a printer attached to your computer is having problems or when other things happen that could keep users from attaching or staying attached to your computer.

Services

In Windows NT, special types of applications can run as background tasks. These applications are *services,* programs that can run independent of a user logon, meaning that they start when Windows NT starts, before the user logon screen even appears. As a result, services are always available to the system and any running applications. Services are usually launched by Windows NT or other applications automatically rather than manually by a user.

A Windows NT service may provide support for any one of a number of system functions, including network-related features such as the capability for the computer to function as a server or workstation, provide network print spooling, or use various Application Program Interfaces (API), such as NetBIOS or DCOM (Network DDE). Other services provide support for miscellaneous Windows NT features, such as UPS communication support and the capability to automatically execute commands at specific times during the day.

Although a user doesn't need to log on to the system in order for a service to run, services themselves must log on to the system with a valid user account. The user account also must have all the privileges and user rights the service requires to perform its functions (that is, membership in the correct local groups with the necessary user rights assigned). Normally, a special user account called *LocalSystem* (the system account) is used for this purpose, but some services may require other user accounts as well.

To manage Windows NT Services:

1. Click the Start button. The Start menu appears.

2. Point to Settings on the Start menu. The Settings menu appears.

3. Click Control Panel. The Control Panel window appears.

4. Double-click the Services icon in the Control Panel. The Services dialog box appears.

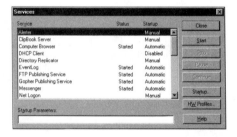

A default set of services is automatically set up and configured based on the installation choices made during Windows NT Setup. The following table lists these default services along with a description of the service's purpose.

Service	What It Does
Alerter	Notifies selected network users or computers of administrative alerts that occur on one computer.
Clipbook Server	Supports the NT Clipbook Viewer application, allowing clipbook pages to be viewed and used by other computers on a network.
Computer Browser	Creates and maintains a list of computers currently available on the network.
DHCP Client	Sends a request on the network to obtain a valid TCP/IP address from a Dynamic Host Control Protocol server on the network. Also, renews that address on a periodic basis to ensure that the address is still valid.
Directory Replicator	Provides the ability to replicate directories and their contained files between computers on a network.
Event Log	Maintains an *audit trail* of all events related to services, devices, applications, security, and so on and records the events in files called event logs.
Messenger	Transmits the messages sent by users, applications or the Alerter service (*see* Alerter).
Net Logon	Participates in security and is responsible for the authentication of user account logons in Windows NT domains.
Network DDE	Responsible for transporting and providing security for network DDE (Dynamic Data Exchange) conversations, which are data-sharing communications channels between applications.
Network DDE DSDM	Responsible for managing Network DDE conversations (*see* Network DDE).
NT LM Security Support Provider	Provides Windows NT-type security to certain RPC (Remote Procedure Call) applications (*see* Remote Procedure Call Service).
OLE	Provides OLE (Object Linking and Embedding) capabilities in Windows NT.
Plug and Play	Provides support for PC Card (PCMCIA) devices.
Remote Procedure Call Locator	Allows applications across a network to use the Microsoft RPC name service. The locator service maintains a database containing the names of currently running RPC server applications. RPC servers register with this service, and RPC client applications request a list of current RPC server names from the service.
Remote Procedure Call Service	Provides the foundation of the RPC (Remote Procedure Call) subsystem in Windows NT.
Schedule	Enables commands to be scheduled to run at a specific date and time using the Windows NT AT command (*see* Automating with the Schedule Service).
Server	Provides file and printer sharing capabilities, as well as named pipe and RPC support.

Service	What It Does
Spooler	Responsible for print spooling services (print queues) in Windows NT.
TCP/IP NetBIOS Helper	Enables use of the NetBIOS API with the TCP/IP network protocol.
Telephony Service	Provides the Windows NT telephony-related services and the Telephony API (TAPI) used by TAPI-aware applications.
UPS	Manages and monitors an uninterruptible power supply to the computer.
Workstation	Provides network connections and communications; the Windows NT redirector.

Hardware profiles

A final option in the Service icon is the ability to enable or disable particular services in different hardware profiles that you define on your Windows NT computer. This option is handy in situations in which different hardware configurations for your computer (for example, a laptop not connected to a networked docking station) require a different set of services. You can enable and disable services in each hardware profile on a case-by-case basis.

To view and modify how a particular service is configured in the hardware profiles on a Windows NT computer:

1. Select the service name by clicking its name in the Services dialog box.

2. Click the H<u>W</u> Profiles button. A window appears for the selected service showing all the currently defined hardware profiles on this computer and the service's configuration in each profile (enabled or disabled).

3. Change the configuration of this service with individual profiles by selecting the profile name in the display and then clicking either the <u>E</u>nable or the <u>D</u>isable button. The status column reflects the current configuration for the service in each profile. Repeat this step for each of the profiles for which you wish to enable or disable the service. After you're finished, click the OK button.

Managing services

The Service dialog box also enables you to stop, pause, or start Windows NT services when necessary (the service is no longer desired or has stopped functioning properly and needs to be restarted, and so on). Note that the buttons Start, Stop, Pause, and Continue enable you to control the service.

Starting a service runs the service application and makes it available to other processes that require it. Stopping a service terminates it and removes it from memory. Pausing is normally done if you need to stop a service, but you cannot immediately stop it because other users are connected to the service (for example, the Server service). In these cases, pause the service, wait until all users are disconnected, and then stop the service. This approach works because pausing causes the service to stop allowing further connections to it but doesn't disconnect active users. If for some reason you decide you want to restart a service after pausing it, you may choose to continue the paused service. (*Note:* Some services cannot be paused. If you select a service that cannot be paused, the Pause button will be inactive.)

To start, stop, pause, or continue services using the Services icon:

1. Open the Services dialog box from the Control Panel window by double-clicking the Services icon.

2. Click the name of the service you want to start, stop, or pause. The status column to the right of the service name informs you of the current status (started, paused, or blank, which indicates the service is not running).

3. Click the button at right for the function you want to perform on the service: Start, Stop, Pause, or Continue. If you are starting a service that requires additional information to start, enter those parameters in the Startup Parameters: text box at the bottom of the Services dialog box.

If backslash characters are required for the parameter(s), two should be entered for the parameter to be interpreted correctly (single backslashes are interpreted as an Escape character, not a slash character).

You see a window containing an animated timer and a message that Windows NT is attempting to perform the selected operation on the service. If the operation is successful, the status column next to the service name reflects the service's new state.

Occasionally, Windows NT can't perform an operation (stop, start, and so on) to a service because the service is no longer responding to the system. In these cases, Windows NT notifies you that the

service did not respond to the request. These situations sometimes require that you shut down and restart your system to solve
the problem.

Setting service startup options

In addition to having the ability to start and stop services, you can
control what state services are in when Windows NT initially
loads, by using the Service dialog box.

To set the startup state for a service, select the service name in
the list of services and click the Startup button on the right. Three
startup options are available for any service and are described in
the following table.

Click This Option	To Do This
Automatic	The service starts automatically when Windows NT starts.
Manual	The service isn't started at Windows NT startup; instead, it runs on demand when the service is requested by a user, application, or dependent service.
Disabled	The service is disabled and cannot be started.

Changing the startup state of a service doesn't affect the service's
current operational state (clicking Disabled doesn't stop the
service); only the next startup is affected. To change the operation
state of a service, use the aforementioned Start, Stop, Pause, and
Continue actions.

To change the startup state for a Windows NT service:

1. Open the Service dialog box by double-clicking the Services
   icon in the Control Panel.

2. In the Service dialog box, select the service with the startup
   state you wish to change.

3. Click the Startup button. The Service dialog box appears.

4. Select the startup type for this service in the Startup Type box: Automatic, Manual, or Disabled.

5. If required, select a user account for the service to log on with in the Log On As box. The default choice is normally the System Account, which uses the special Windows NT LocalSystem user account. If you want the service to provide a user interface to the currently logged-on user, check the Allow Service to Interact with Desktop check box. If a regular NT user account is chosen, the password for that account also needs to be entered in the Password box and again in the Confirm Password box. After you are finished, click the OK button.

Stopping the server service

When using Windows NT on a network, be careful when stopping network-related services because they may be in use by others. The Server service, in particular, should be stopped with caution because the Server service controls (among other things) access to shared files on the Windows NT computer. Because stopping this service immediately disconnects all connected users, data loss may result if users with open files are connected when the server is stopped.

If it becomes necessary to stop the Server service:

1. Open the Service dialog box by double-clicking the Services icon in the Control Panel.

2. Find the Server service in the Service column and click its name to select it.

3. Click the Pause button on the right to pause the service. Windows NT presents a window with a message stating that it is attempting to pause the service. When this happens, the status of the Server service should change from Started to Paused. The Paused state prevents new users from establishing connections with the computer.

4. Using whatever means you choose, notify all users connected to your computer that you are bringing down your computer, and they should close all open files by a specified time. For example, depending on your environment, you may notify them verbally, via e-mail, the Windows NT Chat application, or the more immediate NET SEND command from a DOS box. To send a message to all users in this manner, type **NET SEND *** **"<message>"** and replace the <message> with your message to users notifying them of the imminent shutdown and the amount of time they have to disconnect (the asterisk character stands for all users).

NT users must have the Messenger service already started to receive a message sent via NET SEND, and Windows for Workgroups or Windows 95 users must have the WinPopup program running.

After all users have disconnected, you may safely stop the paused Server service.

Even though pausing the server service prevents ordinary users from making new connections to the computer, users who are members of the Administrators group can continue to make connections.

Sounds

Users with sound boards installed in their Windows NT computers can configure system sounds with the Control Panel Sounds icon. You can customize which sound files (.WAV format files) are played for different events in Windows NT.

 To manage Sounds:

1. Click the Start button. The Start menu appears.

2. Point to Settings on the Start menu. The Settings menu appears.

3. Click Control Panel. The Control Panel window appears.

4. Double-click the Sounds icon in the Control Panel. The Sounds Properties dialog box appears.

The Sounds Properties dialog box has three main sections: Events, Sound, and Schemes. The Events window lists all the programs capable of assigning sounds to events. By default, this list includes Windows, Windows Explorer, Media Player, and Sound Recorder. Within each of these applications is listed all the different event types to which you can assign sounds. Use the up and down scroll bars at the right of the dialog box to view additional programs and program event types.

The sounds section of the Sounds Properties dialog box enables you to listen to sounds that you want to assign to events in the Events box.

To preview a sound file:

1. Select an event from the Events box to assign a sound to.

2. Select the sound file from the Name drop-down list box. Optionally, you can click the Browse button and, using an Explorer-like window, select a sound that is located on a disk drive.

3. Click the Play button to the right of the sound file's name and icon display (the Play button has a right-pointing triangle inside of it).

To stop playing a sound, click the Stop button (the button with a square inside).

To get details on the current sound file listed in the Name box, click the Details button. This action displays a variety of information about the sound file, including the audio format of the file, the length of the sound's playback time, and any copyright information.

Windows NT comes with various schemes of sounds already created. A *scheme* is a group of sounds that belong together and that have already been assigned to events. For example, you can use sounds from the jungle and sounds of a robot. You can select one of these schemes from the Scheme drop-down list box. Or you can assign sounds to different events and then click the Save As button to save your grouping of sounds as a scheme.

System

The Control Panel System icon enables you to view and manage a variety of parameters of your Windows NT computer, such as performance, hardware and user profiles, and general system information.

To manage Windows NT System Properties:

1. Click the Start button. The Start menu appears.

2. Point to Settings on the Start menu. The Settings menu appears.

3. Click Control Panel. The Control Panel window appears.

4. Double-click the System icon in the Control Panel. The System Properties dialog box appears.

The System Properties dialog box contains six tabs for making changes to the System Properties. The tabs are described in the next sections.

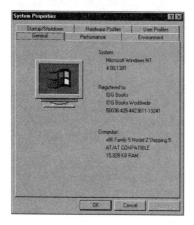

Environment

The Environment tab is used to view and change Windows NT environment variables. MS-DOS users may remember that DOS-provided commands such as the SET command for setting environment variables; Windows NT allows for the graphical configuration of such settings using the System icon.

When Windows NT boots, it also reads the currently defined environment variables (using DOS environment commands such as SET and PATH) from the MS-DOS AUTOEXEC.BAT file (if one exists), to maintain compatibility for older applications on systems upgraded from DOS-based environments.

Two types of environment variables are displayed here: System Variables and User Variables (for the current user). System variables are system-wide, user-independent settings, and user variables affect only the currently logged-on user.

To change either type of variable, click the variable name where it appears in the window. This action places the variable name and value in their respective boxes at the bottom of the window. You may then change the name and/or value for that variable. After you are finished, click the S̲et button. To completely delete a variable and its value, click the variable name and click the D̲elete button. To add a new variable, type the variable name in the V̲ariable text box, as well as what the variable should equate to in the Va̲lue text box. Then click the S̲et button.

General

The General tab shows basic information about the Windows NT system. This information includes the version of Windows NT 4 (the build number is the number displayed after 4.00), the registered owner's name and organization name, the software's serial number, and information on the type of computer Windows NT is being run on, such as CPU type and total amount of system RAM. Note that this information cannot be changed; it is for display only.

Hardware Profiles

The Hardware Profiles tab is an important new feature of Windows NT 4 that enables you to define multiple startup hardware configurations for a single Windows NT system (this feature also exists in Windows 95). For example, you may want Windows NT to start a different set of services and device drivers depending on which hardware is present on your system. Laptop users are the primary reason for the inclusion of this feature; their hardware settings often change due to the presence of different PC Card/PCMCIA devices or a docking station.

Hardware profiles tell which drivers to load when the system's hardware configuration changes. Depending on your system, Windows NT may or may not automatically detect these configuration changes when the system is started. If Windows NT is not able to determine the correct profile to use for a given configuration, you are presented with a list of choices. The default choice and the amount of time elapsed before Windows NT makes a predetermined choice are controlled by the option buttons at the bottom of the tab. The defined profiles are also given a preference order in the Available Hardware Profiles window, with the top-most profile given the highest preference. The position of a particular hardware profile in the preference list may be changed by selecting the profile name and clicking either the up or down arrow buttons.

To direct Windows NT to wait indefinitely for user selection of a hardware profile choice, select the Wait i̲ndefinitely for user selection check box. Otherwise, select the Wait for u̲ser selection check box and enter (in seconds) how long the system should wait before selecting the highest-order preference in the profile list.

After you define your Hardware Profiles, you need to use the Devices and Services Control Panel icons to select which drivers should be loaded for each hardware profile. You can enable and disable devices and services on a case-by-case basis in each hardware profile.

To view the properties of a particular hardware profile, select the profile from the Available Hardware Profiles window and then click Properties. The Properties dialog box appears with tabs that enable you to tell Windows NT whether this is a portable computer, what the docking state (if applicable) of the computer is, and whether network devices and services should be disabled for that profile.

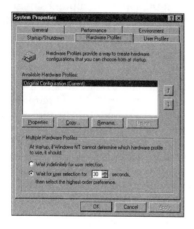

You also may copy one profile to another by selecting the profile to copy and choosing Copy. To rename a profile, select the profile and choose Rename. To delete the profile, choose Delete.

Performance

The Performance tab, as its name implies, enables you to manage performance-related aspects of your Windows NT system. One advantage of Windows NT is that it is a self-optimizing operating system — that is, it monitors certain elements of itself, such as disk performance, and makes adjustments to itself. Therefore, Windows NT requires little or no adjustment to achieve optimum performance.

Despite this, you may want to adjust aspects of the Windows NT performance, such as how Windows NT prioritizes the execution of foreground versus background applications. This aspect may be adjusted using the Application Performance section of the Performance tab. A sliding bar is provided, which has a settings range of None to Maximum. Set the bar to Maximum (the default setting) for the best response time for foreground applications. Set the bar to an in-between setting to provide background programs better response time but still give preference to the application running in the foreground. Setting the bar to None gives all programs (foreground and background) an equal amount of processor time.

The Virtual Memory section of the Performance tab enables you to control the size of the Windows NT paging file, which is stored in a file (or files) called PAGEFILE.SYS in a drive's Root folder. This window also displays the current total size of the system paging file. The paging file can be a single file or multiple files stored across different hard disks and partitions. All of the currently defined paging files added together are collectively referred to as the Windows NT paging file.

The paging file is an extremely important aspect of the Windows NT operating system and controls the amount of hard disk space that may be used by Windows NT as virtual memory. The size of your virtual memory combined with the amount of RAM that is installed in your computer makes up the total amount of memory that Windows NT has for you to use while running applications.

To manage your Windows NT paging file, click the Change button in the Virtual Memory section of the Performance tab to display the Virtual Memory dialog box.

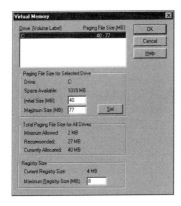

You must be logged on as a member of the Administrators group to make changes to your paging file.

By using this dialog box, you can control where the paging file is placed and what size it will be. The top of the dialog box displays a window containing each of your system's disk partitions and the current size of the paging file on each partition. During installation, Windows NT creates a paging file on one disk partition (usually your Windows NT system partition), which is automatically set to the minimum recommended size if that amount of disk space is available. You may choose to enlarge the size of the paging file or spread the paging file across multiple disk partitions.

For best paging file performance, you should spread the paging file across multiple physical hard disks (not multiple partitions on the same disk, which doesn't provide any advantage), preferably those that are not heavily accessed by other system functions. Also, whenever possible, set your paging file (or total of all paging files) to a minimum of 40MB.

Two aspects control the size of a paging file: Initial Size and Maximum Size. The Initial Size is the starting size of the paging file, which should be determined using the following formula: total physical RAM plus 11MB (the result is the default set by Windows NT). Also, keep in mind that the Windows NT Workstation requires a minimum of approximately 22MB. If system RAM plus 12MB is less than 22MB, increase the size of the paging file until the total of the system RAM plus the paging file size is at east 22MB. This action ensures that your paging file is at least a minimum size that is appropriate for your system.

Windows NT is also capable of dynamically adjusting the paging file size if necessary during the system's operation. The Maximum Size setting is the largest size that the paging file may grow to. To change the size of either figure for a particular drive or create a new paging file on a drive, select the drive on which you want to create or adjust a paging file. Then, enter the numbers in megabytes (MB) in the appropriate boxes, and click the Set button to commit the changes. The paging file changes you set take effect immediately.

The NT Registry size is the final item set by using the Performance tab. The Registry is the Windows NT configuration database, which is the central location for virtually every setting for Windows NT and 32-bit Windows applications. This section displays the current Registry size and enables you to set a Maximum Registry Size, the maximum size in megabytes (MB), that the Registry can occupy on the disk. Increasing this figure neither forces the Registry to allocate this space nor guarantees that this much space will be available later on.

Startup/Shutdown

The Startup/Shutdown tab allows you to configure 1) which operating system should be the default operating system, if you have installed another operating system on the same computer besides Windows NT, and 2) what Windows NT should do if it encounters an error when it starts.

If you have multiple operating system choices on your Windows NT Boot Loader menu, this tab is where you tell Windows NT which operating system to load by default at startup and how long to wait before selecting the default choice. Select the operating system choice from the Startup list and enter the number of seconds to wait in the Show list for box.

The Recovery section of the tab tells Windows NT how to behave when a STOP error occurs. Occasionally, you may receive a STOP error (also known by veteran Windows NT users as a "Blue Screen of Death," so named for its screen color and severity). This error occurs when a major system malfunction is encountered during Windows NT operation. You may control what happens after a STOP error by checking the various boxes listed in this section. Click the box next to Write an event to the system log to have Windows NT log an event for the STOP, which may be viewed using the Event Viewer application.

To direct Windows NT to send an alert message to all users/ computers set to receive alerts, check Send an administrative alert (the list of users/computers receiving such alerts is definable using the Server icon). To have a memory dump containing a contents of system memory at the time of the STOP error recorded to a file, check the Write debugging information to box. If you want the file automatically overwritten if it already exists, check the Overwrite any existing file box. Enabling this option can be helpful to developers diagnosing the cause of a STOP error; occasionally, application developers or Microsoft may request this file to aid them in determining the source of a problem.

Finally, check the Automatically reboot box to direct your system to automatically reboot after a STOP error occurs.

Checking the automatic reboot option on a system acting as file or print server on a network is a good idea; if the system experiences the STOP error while the administrator is away, it automatically reboots and continues to provide services to network users after it restarts.

User Profiles

In addition to multiple hardware configuration profiles, having multiple profiles for different users on a Windows NT system is also possible. The User Profiles tab contains desktop settings, preferences, and other user-centric information.

Three types of user profiles exist in Windows NT. *Local* user profiles are user-managed profiles stored locally on your computer (the filename is NTUSER.DAT). *Roaming* user profiles are server-based profiles that can follow users as they move to different machines (the file extension is .USR). Finally, depending on your network configuration, a user account may be assigned a *mandatory* profile by the Network Administrator, a server-based profile that cannot be changed by the user (the file extension is .MAN).

After a valid Windows NT user account is created for the user by the Network Administrator, and after the user first logs on, a user profile is automatically created for that user. If you want to create additional user profiles and assign them to specific users, you can use the User Profiles tab.

This tab displays a list of all profiles that are currently stored on the computer, for all users who have accessed the computer. To select a profile name to manage, first select the profile in the displayed list. To delete the profile, click the Delete button.

To change the type of the user profile between local and roaming, click the Change Type button. The Change Type dialog box opens. Select either Local profile or Roaming profile. For roaming profiles that may be accessed over slow connections (modem connections using remote access), be sure to also click the Use cached profile on slow connections box. This action ensures that in situations where access to the server storing the roaming profile is slow, the local copy of the profile is used instead of copying the roaming profile from the server to the local machine.

Finally, to copy the currently selected profile to a new location, click the Copy To button. The Copy To dialog box opens. Enter the new location to which you want to copy the profile. You also may select the new location by clicking the Browse button. If you want to assign permissions to use the new profile to a particular user or user group, click the Change button in the Permitted to use section of the Copy To dialog box. You can select the user or group name who should be granted permission to use the profile.

Tape Devices

 Windows NT contains built-in support for tape drives from a variety of different manufacturers. The Tape Devices icon of the Control Panel enables you to manage the tape devices installed on your system.

To manage Tape devices:

1. Click the Start button. The Start menu appears.

2. Point to Settings on the Start menu. The Settings menu appears.

3. Click Control Panel. The Control Panel window appears.

4. Double-click the Tape Devices icon in the Control Panel. The Tape Devices dialog box appears.

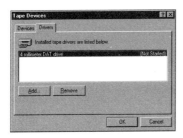

The Tape Devices dialog box contains two tabs: the Devices tab and the Drivers tab. The Devices tab shows the tape drives currently installed on your system. To get the properties of a tape drive, select the drive and click the Properties button. To have Windows NT attempt to automatically detect your tape drive, click the Detect button. If a tape drive is detected, Windows NT installs support for the device.

If your device is not detected (because Windows NT failed to recognize it, or you are using a drive with third-party drivers), you may use the Drivers tab to install support for the drive manually.

To add a tape drive to your Windows NT configuration:

1. Double-click the Tape Devices icon in the Control Panel. The Tape Devices dialog box appears.

2. Click the Drivers tab.

3. Click the Add button. The Install Driver dialog box appears, which lists all supported tape drive manufacturers and models.

4. From the list, select the manufacturer and model of your tape drive. If your drive is not listed but the drive came with a Windows NT 4 driver from the manufacturer, click the Have Disk button.

5. Windows NT prompts you for either the Windows NT 4 CD-ROM or vendor-supplied diskette (if using the Have Disk option) containing support for the tape device.

6. After you are finished, you are required to restart your system to complete the installation.

Alternatively, if you want to remove an installed tape drive from the list, select the device and click the Remove button. Windows NT asks you to confirm removal of the device.

After support for your tape device is installed, you can use the Windows NT Backup application and other Windows NT backup programs containing tape device support.

Telephony

The Telephony icon of the Control Panel controls your Telephony settings in Windows NT.

To manage Windows NT Telephony:

1. Click the Start button. The Start menu appears.

2. Point to Settings on the Start menu. The Settings menu appears.

3. Click Control Panel. The Control Panel window appears.

4. Double-click the Telephony icon in the Control Panel. The Dialing Properties dialog box appears. The dialog box has two tabs, My Locations and Telephony Drivers.

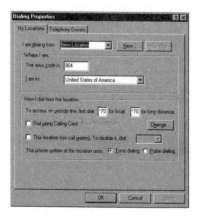

The Telephony Drivers tab enables you to view and manage the list of currently installed Telephony drivers. Drivers may be added, removed, or configured in this tab.

The most common Telephony driver in Windows NT is the Unimodem Service Provider driver, which is automatically installed when you set up a modem (or fax modem) using the Control Panel Modems icon. This setup allows Telephony-based applications to communicate with your modem. The other driver you should see is the TAPI Kernel-Mode Service Provider driver, which provides TAPI support in the Windows NT environment. If you purchase Telephony hardware or software that includes additional NT Telephony drivers required to support the device, you may add them using the Telephony Drivers tab.

To add a Telephony driver to your Windows NT configuration:

1. Open the Dialing Properties dialog box by double-clicking the Telephony icon in the Control Panel.

2. Click the Telephony Drivers tab.

3. Click the Add button. The Add Driver dialog box appears, listing all Telephony drivers shipped with Windows NT (currently only the Unimodem Service Provider driver).

4. Select the driver you want to install or if you have a vendor-supplied NT 4 Telephony driver disk, click the Have Disk button.

5. Windows NT prompts you for either the Windows NT 4 CD-ROM or the vendor-supplied diskette (if using the Have Disk option) containing support for the tape device.

To remove a Telephony driver, select the driver from the displayed list and click the Remove button. To configure the driver, click the Configure button, which displays the configuration dialog box for that driver.

The My Locations tab tells Windows NT the locations where you will use Telephony software. You can set different dialing properties for each location, such as: area code, country, calling card, and outside line access information. This screen is identical to the Dialing Properties screen found in the Modems icon and references the same configuration information.

Part X

Keeping Tabs on Windows NT

Windows NT is a powerful operating system that can handle many tasks. One of its powerful features is the capability to manage multiple users. Windows NT enables you to administer how multiple people can use the same computer, or access files and printers from a computer. Equally important, if not more important than administering users, is administering the computer itself. Windows NT provides the tools that you need to administer performance on the computer, and to protect the data that you store on the computer.

In this part . . .

- ✔ **Backing up and restoring information**
- ✔ **Viewing events**
- ✔ **Monitoring performance**
- ✔ **Working with groups**

Administration Tools

You can use a number of tools to administer your Windows NT computer. You can use these tools to assign users, specify the access permissions that users have, monitor the performance of the computer, view events that occur at the computer, diagnose Windows NT, backup and restore data, and manage hard-disk space in the computer.

Not just anyone who logs on to the computer can administer the computer. For a person to be fully capable of administering any part of a Windows NT computer, he or she must be declared an administrator. When Windows NT was first installed on your computer, a special administrator user ID had to be created. When administering your computer, logging on as this account is best.

What are the tools that you can use to administer your Windows NT computer? The following table lists these tools and what you can do with them:

Administration Tool	What It's For
User Manager	Enables you to add, change, and remove users and groups of users that can access the computer, as well as set levels of access permissions for users and groups of users.
Windows NT Diagnostics	Displays information about the current operation of the computer such as memory usage, available resources, and network statistics. This information is helpful for troubleshooting system problems.
Performance Monitor	Enables you to monitor the performance of the system. This feature is useful for determining what components in your computer may keep your PC from performing at its greatest potential.
Event Viewer	Allows you to view events that happen on your computer. Events include: a print command to the printer, a failure of a Windows NT software component, and a logon to your computer. Messages are cautions, warnings, and information.
Disk Administrator	Enables you to add a hard disk to your computer, prepare your hard disk for use with Windows NT, or view current disk usage. Also offers the capability of using multiple disks together, working as one hard disk.
Backup	Lets you protect your data by backing up and restoring files from your hard drive to a tape drive.
Remote Access Admin	Lets you control and monitor remote access services. You can stop, start, or pause remote access, and you can send messages to users.

Backup

The ability to back up your data is critical. Windows NT contains an easy-to-use backup program. Unlike other backup programs, however, Windows NT Backup does not allow you to back up to disk drives. Instead, Windows NT Backup supports only tape drives. For backing up large amounts of data, however, using a tape drive is much more convenient and reliable.

To start the backup:

1. Click the Start button. The Start menu opens.

2. Point to Programs. The Programs menu opens.

3. Point to Administrative Tools (Common). The Administrative Tools menu opens.

4. Click Backup. The Backup window opens.

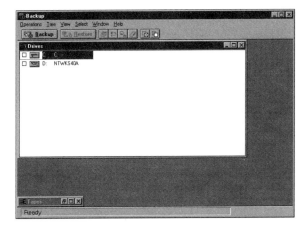

Backing up files

To back up files, you must select the files, directories, or drives to back up, select a tape drive to back up to, and then start backing up.

To select files to back up:

1. Start Windows NT Backup.

2. Insert a tape in the drive.

3. Open the Drives window by either clicking it or by choosing Window⇨1 Drives.

4. Select the drives, directories, or files to back up as follows:

To select an entire drive, mark the Drives check box in the Drives window.

To select directories of files, double-click the Drive icon containing the directories to back up. A window appears showing the contents of the drive. Mark the check box of the directories to back up. Or, double-click a directory to view its contents, and mark the check box of the individual directories or files contained within the open directory.

When you select a file or directory to back up, you mark the check box. If you select a directory or a file within another directory, the check box of the parent drive or directory is also marked but is colored gray. This color indicates that some of the contents of the directory is checked, but not the whole directory. This marking assures you that Windows NT Backup preserves the directory structure of the drive as well as backs up your files.

To back up files:

1. After you have selected the files to back up, choose Operations⇨Backup or click the Backup button on the toolbar. The Backup Information dialog box appears.

2. Make all settings in the dialog box and then click OK to start the backup. The Backup Status dialog box displays, showing you the progress of your backup.

3. After the backup is complete, remove and store your tape in a safe place.

You can set a number of options in the Backup Information dialog box. The following table describes these options.

Backup Options	Description
Tape Name	Type a name of up to 32 characters that describes this tape.
Operation	Select Append to add the backup files to the existing tape or select Replace to overwrite the contents of the tape with the new backup set.
Verify After Backup	Check this box to compare the files that you have backed up to the tape with the files on the disk.
Backup Local Registry	Back up the Windows NT Registry along with the files that you have selected.
Restrict Access to Owner Or Administrator	Prevent anyone other than the owner of the file or the administrator of the Windows NT computer from restoring the files.

Backup Options	*Description*
Hardware Compression	If your backup drive enables data compression, check this box to use hardware compression. This option enables more data to be stored on a tape.
Backup Set Information	Type a name that describes the backup set that you are creating. A tape can contain more than one backup set.
Backup Type	Click the option button indicating the type of backup you want to perform.
Logging Type	Click the Full Detail option button to log all drives, directories, and files that are backed up. Click the Summary Only option button to log only a summary of the drives, directories, and files that you back up. Click the Don't Log option button to prevent any logging.
Log File	In this text box, type the name of the log file to create.

Cataloging a tape

When you back up files, Windows NT Backup creates a catalog of files on the tape. The catalog is stored on your hard disk. If a catalog for a tape that you want to restore from is missing, you can recreate the catalog by telling Windows NT Backup to read the tape and create the catalog.

To create a catalog of a tape:

1. Start Windows NT Backup.

2. Insert a tape in the tape drive.

3. Select Tapes window by either clicking it or by choosing Window⇨2 Tapes.

4. Choose Operations⇨Catalog. The Catalog Status dialog box appears. Windows NT Backup begins searching the tape for catalogs. The status of the search displays in the Catalog Status dialog box. Catalogs appear in the Tapes window. You can click the Abort button in the Catalog Status dialog box to stop cataloging.

5. After all catalogs for the inserted backup tape appear in the Window, you can double-click the catalog that you intend to use.

You use the catalog to select files to restore.

Restoring files

You must admit, a backup program is only as good as its capability to restore files. Restoring files is a similar process to backing up files. You must select the tape to restore from, select the files, directories, or drives to restore, and then start restoring.

To select files to restore:

1. Start Windows NT Backup.

2. Select the Tape window by either clicking it or by choosing Window⇨2 Tapes.

3. Insert your tape and then choose Operations⇨Catalog. The catalogs contained on the tape are displayed in the Tapes window.

4. Mark the check box of the drives, directories, or files to restore.

To select an entire drive, mark the Drives check box in the Drives window.

To select directories of files, double-click the Drive icon containing the directories to backup. A window appears, showing the contents of the drive. Mark the check box of the directories to backup. Or, double-click a directory to view its contents, and mark the check box of the individual directories or files contained within the open directory.

To start restoring files:

1. After you have selected files to restore, choose Operations⇨ Restore or click the Restore button on the toolbar. The Restore Information dialog box appears on the screen.

2. Check the setting you desire in the Restore Information dialog box and then click OK. The Restore Status dialog box appears, displaying the status of your restoration.

The Restore Information dialog box contains a number of settings that you can make before restoring. These settings are described in the following table:

Restore Options	Description
Alternate Path	The original path of files that you back up is preserved. If you restore a file, the file returns to its original path. However, you can select a different path for the file.

Restore Options	Description
Restore Local Registry	Mark this check box to restore the Windows NT Registry. Be careful when you use this option, because you can overwrite changes that have been made to the registry.
Restore File Permissions	Mark this check box to restore file permissions when you restore the files. File permissions indicate who can and cannot access the file.
Verify After Restore	Mark this check box to verify that files are restored correctly.
Logging Type	Click the Full Detail option button to log all restored drives, directories, and files. Click the Summary Only option button to log only a summary of the drives, directories, and files that you restore. Click the Don't Log option button to prevent any logging.
Log File	In this text box, type the name of the log file to create.

Event Viewer

As Windows NT operates, events occur. Events are any significant occurrence that takes place in the Windows NT system. Events vary from informational to critical. Events are recorded in three basic categories, so you can view three basic kinds of logs with Event Viewer — system events, security events, and application events.

To start the Event Viewer:

1. Click the Start button. The Start menu opens.

2. Point to Programs. The Programs menu opens.

3. Point to Administrative Tools (Common). The Administrative Tools menu opens.

4. Click Event Viewer. The Event Viewer window opens.

Changing log settings

You can alter the amount of information that is contained in the log files in two ways. One method is by changing the maximum size that the log file can be. The other way is by indicating whether or not events in the log can be overwritten.

To change the log settings:

1. Start the Event Viewer.

2. Choose Log⇨Log Settings. The Event Log Settings dialog box opens.

3. Make the appropriate log settings and then click OK to save the changes.

The following table describes the settings found in the Event Log Settings dialog box:

Settings Option	Description
Change Settings for	Use this drop-down list box to select the log whose settings you want to change.
Maximum Log Size	Set the maximum size (in kilobytes) that the selected log can be.
Event Log Wrapping	Enables you to define whether additional events can be recorded by deleting older events in the log. Contains three options. Select the Overwrite Events as Needed option button to continuously add new events by overwriting old events. Select the Overwrite Events Older than option button and select a number of days to enable events older than the specified number of days to be overwritten by new events. Select the Do Not Overwrite Events (Clear Log Manually) option button to avoid overwriting any events.

Clearing the event log

You can clear each log, enabling you to purge unnecessary information in a log or collect new information in a log. To clear a log:

1. Start the Event Viewer.

2. Select the log to clear by choosing Log and either System, Security, or Application.

3. Choose Log⇨Clear All Events. The Clear Event Log dialog box appears, asking if you want to save the log.

4. Click the Yes button to save the log before clearing it, or click the No button to clear the log. If you click Yes, the Save As dialog box appears. Type a name in the File name text box and then click the Save button.

5. In the next Clear Event Log dialog box, you are alerted that clearing an event log is irreversible. Click the No button to abandon clearing the log, or click the Yes button to continue.

If you selected Yes, the log that you are viewing is cleared of old entries. New entries will begin appearing in that log.

Remember: If you choose to clear all events, you are clearing events only for the current log. So, for example, if you are viewing the Application Log and you clear all events, you clear events only for the Application Log. The System Log and the Security Log are unaffected.

Filtering events

Many types of events are recorded in each of the event logs. However, you may find it necessary to filter out unnecessary log entries to view log entries that pertain only to your current interest. For example, you may be concerned only with events that occurred in a two-hour period on a certain day. In that case, you can filter out all other events.

To create a filter:

1. Start the Event Viewer.

2. Select the Log to view.

3. Choose <u>V</u>iew⇨Fi<u>l</u>ter Events. The Filter dialog box appears.

4. Make the settings that you desire for filtration and then click OK.

The following table lists the selections that you can make from the Filter dialog box.

Filter Parameter	Description
View From	Select the <u>F</u>irst Event option button to begin displaying at the first event in the log or select the Events <u>O</u>n option button and enter a date and time for the first event in the log to display.
View Through	Select the <u>L</u>ast Event option button to display to the last event in the log or select the Events O<u>n</u> option button and enter a date and time for the last event in the log to display.
Types	Mark any of the following check boxes to display those types of events: <u>I</u>nformation, <u>W</u>arning, <u>E</u>rror, <u>S</u>uccess Audit, F<u>a</u>ilure Audit.
Source	From this drop-down list box, select the item that creates an event log entry for the type of entry to display.
Category	From this drop-down list box, select the category of event log entry to display.
User	Type the name of the User whose event log entries you want to display.
Computer	Type the name of the computer connecting to this computer whose event log entries you want to display.
Event ID	Type the event ID of the Event Log entries to display.
Clear	Click this button to clear any selections that you have made in the Filter dialog box and return all entries to their default values.

Finding an event

An Event Log can contain hundreds of entries. Finding an event can be quite a task. So, why not take advantage of the computer's ability to quickly search for information?

To find an event:

1. Start the Event Viewer.

2. Select the log to search through.

3. Choose View⇨Find. The Find dialog box appears.

4. Check the settings that you desire to find and then click the Find Next button.

The following table lists the selections that you can make in the Find dialog box:

Find Parameter	Description
Types	Mark any of the following check boxes to display those types of events: Information, Warning, Error, Success Audit, Failure Audit.
Source	From this drop-down list box, select the item that creates an event log entry for the type of entry to find.
Category	From this drop-down list box, select the category of event log entry to find.
User	Type the name of the user whose event log entries you want to find.
Computer	Type the name of the computer connecting to this computer whose event log entries you want to find.
Event ID	Type the event ID of the event log entries you want to find.
Direction	Select either the Up or Down option button to indicate the direction through the log that you want to search.
Clear	Click this button to clear any selections that you have made in the Filter dialog box and return all entries to their default values.

Opening an event

Occasionally, you may need to open an event log that you have previously saved.

To open an event log:

1. Start the Event Viewer.

2. Choose Log⇨Open. The Open dialog box displays on the screen.

3. Select the drive and directory containing the log file and then select the log file.

4. Click the Open button. The Open File Type dialog box appears.

5. From the Open File Type dialog box, select the log to open. Select either the System option button, the Security option button, or the Application option button.

6. Click OK. The log that you selected displays in the Event Viewer.

Saving log files

Log files are limited in size by two factors — by file size and by age of the events. Because of this limitation, events are overwritten as they become old or as the event log reaches its maximum size. You can maintain event logs, however, by saving the log from time to time.

To save a log:

1. Start the Event Viewer.

2. Choose Log➪Save As. The Save As dialog box appears on the screen.

3. Select the drive and directory to save the log file. Type the name for the log file in the File name text box.

4. Click the Save button. The log file is saved.

Selecting a different log

The Event Viewer can display events from the System Log, the Security Log, and the Application Log. To select the log to display, start the Event Viewer, choose the Log menu, and then choose either System, Security, or Application.

Viewing events from a different computer

With the Event Viewer, you can view events from other computers. To view event logs from another computer:

1. Start the Event Viewer.

2. Choose Log➪Select Computer. The Select Computer dialog box displays on the screen.

3. Click the computer to open the Select Computer list box or type the name of a computer in the Computer text box.

4. Click OK. The event logs from the selected computer appear in the Event Viewer.

Performance Monitor

The Performance Monitor is a very powerful software tool that enables you to evaluate the performance of your computer. You can display statistics or graphs that enable you to determine just how well (or how not so well) your Windows NT system is performing.

To start the Performance Monitor:

1. Click the Start button. The Start menu opens.

2. Point to Programs. The Programs menu opens.

3. Point to Administrative Tools (Common). The Administrative Tools menu opens.

4. Click Performance Monitor. The Performance Monitor window opens.

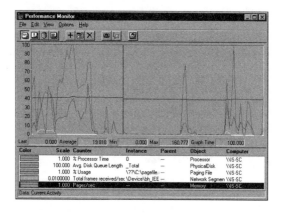

Creating new alert settings

When you are ready to display new or different alert information, you need to remove old settings and create a new alert list. To create new alert settings:

1. Start the Performance Monitor and select View➪Alert.

2. Choose File➪New Alert Settings. Any alerts currently displayed disappear, previously selected settings are removed, and you are ready to display a new alert list using different settings.

Creating a new chart

When you are ready to display new or different charts, you need to remove old settings and create a new chart. To create a new chart:

1. Start the Performance Monitor and select View⇨Chart.

2. Choose File⇨New Chart. Any charts currently displayed disappear, previously selected settings are removed, and you are ready to display a new chart using different settings.

Creating new log settings

When you are ready to display new or different log information, you need to remove old settings and create a new log. To create new log settings:

1. Start the Performance Monitor and select View⇨Log.

2. Choose File⇨New Log Settings. Any logs currently displayed disappear, previously selected settings are removed, and you are ready to display a new log using different settings.

Creating new report settings

When you are ready to display new or different report information, you need to remove old settings and create a new report. To create new report settings:

1. Start the Performance Monitor and select View⇨Report.

2. Choose File⇨New Report Settings. Any report information currently displayed disappears, previously selected settings are removed, and you are ready to display a new report using different settings.

Opening a saved settings file

As you have monitored the performance of Windows NT, you may have created a display that you feel is useful, not just for the moment, but to look at from time to time. So, you may save settings. Of course, if you save settings, you need to be able to re-open the settings.

To open saved settings:

1. Start the Performance Monitor.

2. Choose File⇨Open. The Performance Monitor–File Open dialog box appears.

3. Select the drive and directory that contain the settings file and then select the settings file to open.

4. Click the Open button. The Performance Monitor begins collecting and displaying information based on the settings from the file that you opened.

If you open a settings file but have not saved any settings before opening the file, those unsaved settings are lost without a warning.

Saving settings

As you use Performance Monitor, you find that you view common settings often. Rather than rebuild the settings that you want to view each time you start Performance Monitor, you can save settings that you find useful.

To save settings:

1. Select the settings that you want to view with Performance Monitor.

2. Choose File⇨Save Settings As. The Performance Monitor–Save As dialog box appears.

3. Select the drive and directory where you want to save the settings file.

4. Type the name of the settings file in the File name text box.

5. Click the Save button. The settings are saved and you again view the Performance Monitor. The title bar of the Performance Monitor window displays the new settings filename.

If you make any changes and want to save those changes in an existing file, open the settings file, make the changes that you desire, and choose File⇨Save. The changes are saved in the file that is open.

Changing the view

Performance Monitor offers four different ways to view the performance of Windows NT. You can view a chart, which creates a graph enabling you to graphically see the performance of Windows NT as it occurs. You can choose View Alert, which displays information after it has passed a threshold set by you. You can select Log view, which enables you to capture statistics in a file for a certain period of time, for your evaluation later. You can select the Report view to display the same type of information you view in Chart view, except Performance Monitor displays the values in a report form rather than in a graph form.

To change the view:

1. Start the Performance Monitor.

2. Choose the Yiew menu.

3. From the Yiew menu, choose the view of your choice.

Windows NT offers several quick ways to switch your view. One way is to click one of the View buttons on the toolbar. Another is to press Ctrl+A for the Alert view, Ctrl+C for the Chart view, Ctrl+L for the Log view, or Ctrl+R for the Report view.

Adding items to monitor

To be useful, you need to add items to monitor the view in the Performance Monitor.

To add items to monitor:

1. Start the Performance Monitor.

2. Select the view of your choice.

3. Choose the Edit menu.

4. From the Edit menu, choose the Add To option. The Add to dialog box displays.

5. Select the item to add and then click the Add button. You add as many items from this dialog box as you like.

6. After you are done adding items, click the Done button.

The Add to dialog box varies in appearance depending on the view you are currently using. However, in each case, you select one item to monitor at a time. You can continue adding items until you are finished, and then you close the Add to dialog box.

User Manager

To start the User Manager:

1. Click the Start button. The Start menu opens.

2. Point to Programs. The Programs menu opens.

3. Point to Administrative Tools (Common). The Administrative Tools menu opens.

4. Click User Manager. The User Manager window opens.

Creating a local group

Local groups enable you to group users together for ease of assigning access permissions. Windows NT provides six default groups. You may find it necessary, however, to create other groups for refining the types of permissions. For example, one of the groups already created is called Users. By default, all users are assigned to this group. However, you may want to create two other user groups so that you can customize the types of access permissions that you assign to users. You may allow one group to only read files in a directory, whereas you give the second group access to not only read the files but also to make changes to those files.

To create a local group:

1. Start the User Manager.

2. Choose User⇨New Local Group. The New Local Group dialog box appears on the screen.

3. Type the name of the group in the Group Name text box.

Optionally, type a group description in the Description text box.

4. Add users to the group by clicking the Add button. After the Add Users and Groups dialog box appears, select the users to add, click the Add button, and then click OK.

5. Remove users that you do not want in the group. Select the users to remove from the Members list box and then click the Remove button.

6. Click OK to save the new local group.

Adding users to a local group

Windows NT enables you to group like users together. This arrangement makes assigning access permissions easy. Rather than assign access permissions to each individual user, you assign each user to a group and then give your specific access permissions to that group.

To add users to a local group:

1. Start the User Manager.

2. In the Groups window, double-click the group you want to modify. The Local Group Properties dialog box appears.

3. Click the Add button. The Add Users and Groups dialog box appears.

4. Select the user or users to add to the group from the Names list window and then click the Add button.

5. Click OK to save the changes in the Add Users and Groups dialog box and return to the Local Group Properties dialog box.

6. Click OK to save the changes in the Local Group Properties dialog box.

Changing a user's group

To change a user:

1. Start the User Manager.

2. In the Username list window, double-click the user you want to change. The User Properties dialog box appears.

3. Click the Groups button. The Group Memberships dialog box appears.

4. Add the user to other groups by selecting a group or groups from the Not member of list box and clicking the Add button. Remove the user from groups by selecting the group or groups from the Member of list box and clicking the Remove button.

5. Click the OK button to save changes in the Group Memberships dialog box.

6. Click the OK button to close the User Properties dialog box.

Deleting a local group

You may no longer need a local group. To delete a local group:

1. Start the User Manager.

2. Select the local group to delete from the Groups list box.

3. Choose User⇨Delete or just press the Del key. A warning box appears giving you information about deleting groups.

4. Click OK. Another warning box appears.

5. Click Yes. The group is deleted.

Even though a group contains users, deleting a group does not affect any of the user accounts.

Removing a user from a local group

Windows NT enables you to group like users together. This arrangement makes assigning access permissions easy. Rather than assigning or removing access permissions for each individual user, you assign each user to a group and then give your specific access permissions to that group. To disallow a user from accessing a specific directory, you remove the user from that local group.

To remove users from a local group:

1. Start the User Manager.

2. In the Groups window, double-click the group you want to modify. The Local Group Properties dialog box appears.

3. Select the user or users to remove in the Members list box.

4. Click the Remove button to remove the user or users from the local group.

5. Click OK to save the changes in the Local Group Properties dialog box.

Renaming a user

From time to time, people's names change. Or, you may find out that you misspelled a user's name. Instead of deleting an account, which may have very intricate settings, and creating a new account for a user, you can choose to rename an existing account.

To rename a user:

1. Start the User Manager.

2. Select the user to rename from the Username list box.

3. Choose User⇨Rename. The Rename dialog box appears.

4. In the Change To box, type the new username. This name is not the full name, but rather the user ID that you want to assign to the user. For example, Joan Smith's user ID may be JSmith.

5. Click OK.

Renaming a user changes only the logon ID. To change the user's full name, double-click the user's account, change the full name, and then click OK to save the changes.

Setting user rights

You set user rights to enable a user or a group of users to perform certain tasks, such as backing up files and directories, changing the system time, and shutting down the system.

To set user rights:

1. Start the User Manager.

2. Choose Policies⇨User Rights. The User Rights Policy dialog box opens.

3. From the Rights drop-down list box, select the appropriate user right. To select an advanced user right, click the Show Advanced User Rights check box before you open the Right: drop-down list box.

4. Click the Add button to add users or groups to the right. When you click the Add button, the Add Users and Groups dialog box opens. From this dialog box, select users, click the Add button, and then click OK to return to the User Rights Policy dialog box.

5. Select a user or a group from the Grant To list box and then click the Remove button to remove users so that they do not have the right or privilege listed in the Right: list box.

6. Click OK to close the User Rights Policy dialog box and save changes.

Techie Talk

Authentication: A Windows NT computer goes through this process to make sure that you are who you say you are. After a user logs on to an account on a Windows NT computer, the authentication is performed by that computer. After a user logs on to an account on a Windows NT Server domain, the authentication may be performed by any server of that domain.

Backup Domain Controller: A computer that receives a copy of the Windows NT Server domain's security policy and domain database. The computer uses this information to authenticate network logons.

Browse: Just as you do when you're window shopping, this feature looks through lists of directories, files, user accounts, groups, domains, or computers.

Channel: A Web site designed to deliver content from the Internet to your computer. Just as you do with TV, you tune in or subscribe to a favorite Web site. With channels, the content provider can suggest a schedule for your subscription, or you can customize your own.

Client: A computer that accesses shared-network resources provided by another computer (called a *server*) — usually at no charge to the client, although you may want to set up a service charge to earn extra money.

Clipboard: A temporary storage space within the computer's memory in which you can save text or graphics for later reuse. You place items on the Clipboard by using the Cut or Copy commands within an application. To reuse the Clipboard item, use the Paste command.

Computer Name: A unique name of up to 15 characters that identifies a computer to the network. The name cannot be the same as any other computer or domain name in the network.

Content Advisor: Internet Explorer's way of screening the types of content that your computer can access on the Internet. After you turn on Content Advisor, only rated content that meets or exceeds your criteria can be displayed.

Cursor: The little I-shaped bar that follows you around the screen when you move the mouse. (Cursors can have other shapes. Some are shaped like dinosaurs, for example.)

Directory: Areas on a disk used to store files. Directories are called *folders* in Windows NT 4.

Document: A document is what an application displays in its window. If you're using a word processor, a document may be a letter, memo, fax, or other work.

Domain Controller: Every Windows NT Server domain has a server — the domain controller — that authenticates or validates domain logons and maintains the security policy and the master database for a domain.

Domain Name: The name by which a domain is known to the network.

Domain: For a Windows NT Server, a domain is a collection of computers that share a common account database and security policy. Each domain has a unique name.

Double-click: To click twice very fast, without moving the mouse cursor between clicks.

Drag and drop: A technique (click, hold, drag, release) that allows you to move or copy files or pieces of documents using the mouse.

Event: A happening in Windows NT, such as printing a document or starting a Windows NT service.

FAT: Stands for *file allocation table,* which is a table or list maintained by some operating systems to keep track of the status of various segments or portions of disk space used for file storage.

Folder: You knew folders as directories under DOS. A folder is an area on a disk where files are stored.

Hal (Hardware Abstraction Layer): Enables Windows NT to work with different types of hardware (serves like a mediator between two sides that can't get along).

Icon: Those cute little pictures that litter your desktop. An icon represents programs or data files.

Local Group: Used for security with Windows NT. A local group is comprised of users who have permission to use a Windows NT directory or printer. The term *local* refers to the computer to which the user connects.

Maximize: To enlarge an icon to a window that takes up the entire screen.

Minimize: To shrink a window to an icon that appears on the Taskbar.

MS-DOS-Based Application: An application designed to run with plain ol' MS-DOS. Therefore, the application may not be able to take full advantage of all Windows NT features.

Network: A collection of computers and peripheral devices connected together via cabling, fiber optics, or wireless technologies.

Non-Windows NT Application: An application designed to run with those other operating systems, such as Windows 3.*x,* MS-DOS, OS/2, or POSIX, but not specifically with Windows NT. Note that applications designed to run on Windows 95 *usually* run without a hitch on Windows NT and take full advantage of all the Windows NT features.

NTFS: Stands for Windows *NT file system,* an advanced file system designed to be used specifically by the Windows NT operating system. It supports file system recovery, extremely large storage media, and a slew of other goodies.

Offline Browsing: You can view Web pages without being connected to the Internet, provided that the page is stored locally on your hard drive. This is handy if you don't always have access to the Web when you want to browse Web pages. You might be using your laptop computer at a location that does not provide any network or modem access. Or you might be at home and not want to tie up your only phone line.

Partition: A logical storage element. A partition can be a portion of a hard disk, an entire hard disk, or multiple hard disks that work together to store data.

Password: A unique string of characters that must be provided before a logon or an access is authorized. A password is a security measure used to restrict logons to user accounts and access to computer systems and resources. For Windows NT, a password for a user account can be up to 14 characters and is case sensitive.

Permissions: Assigning a user rights to use a Windows NT file, directory, or printer. These rights include no-access permissions, read-only permissions, change permissions, and full-access permissions.

Print job: A document sent to the printer. A print job is the smallest element that you can move, pause, or delete using the Print Manager.

Profile Assistant: Internet Explorer's way of letting Web sites know who and where you are. Profile assistant can send registration and demographic information to Web sites that require this information so that you don't have to repeatedly enter the same information, such as your address or e-mail name, every time you visit a new Web site. None of this information can be viewed on your computer or shared with others without your permission.

Protocol: Software that follows specific rules to communicate over a network, such as NetBEUI, TCP/IP, and NWLink.

Registry: A secure file that Windows NT uses to write configuration information about itself.

Resource: Any part of a computer system or a network, such as a disk drive, printer, or memory, that can be accessed or used.

Security Certificates: A *certificate* is a statement guaranteeing the identity of a person or the security of a Web site. A *personal certificate* is a kind of guarantee that you are who you say you are. A *Web site certificate* states that a specific Web site is secure and genuine.

Server: In general, a computer that provides shared resources to network users. In some specific cases, *server* refers to a computer that runs a Windows NT Server but is not a primary domain controller or a backup domain controller of a Windows NT domain.

Service: A process that performs a specific system function and often provides an application programming interface (API) for other processes to call.

Share: An element of Windows NT that others are allowed to use, such as printers and directories.

Striped Set: Combining multiple hard-disk partitions to make a large storage area providing high performance. With a striped set, Windows NT splits files that you save across multiple hard disks and reads them back in proper sequence. Writing and reading files in this fashion is very fast, because files can be written and read much more quickly when split across multiple hard disks than they can when written to and read from a single hard disk.

Taskbar: The bar that lists all currently running programs and open folders.

User Account: Consists of all the information that defines a user to Windows NT (similar to a dossier). This information includes the user name and password required for the user to log on, the groups in which the user account has membership, and the rights and permissions the user has for using the system and accessing its resources.

User Name: A unique name identifying a user account to Windows NT. An account's user name cannot be identical to any other group name or user name of its own domain or workgroup.

Volume Set: Combining multiple volumes together to create a large hard-disk storage area. Using the Disk Administrator, you can combine multiple partitions that enable you to store more information than a single hard disk can hold.

Volume: A formatted hard disk partition that either contains files or is ready to contain files.

Windows NT Server: The Windows NT product that provides centralized management and security, advanced fault tolerance, and additional connectivity.

Windows NT Workstation: The Windows NT product that provides operating system and networking functionality for computers without centralized management.

Windows NT: The portable, secure, 32-bit, muscle-bound, preemptive multitasking member of the Microsoft Windows operating system family.

Workgroup: A collection of computers grouped for viewing purposes. A unique name identifies each workgroup.

Workstation: Computers running the Windows NT Workstation operating system are called *workstations*, to distinguish them from computers running Windows NT Server.

Index

IDG BOOKS WORLDWIDE BOOK REGISTRATION

Register
This Book
and Win!

We want to hear from you!

Visit **http://my2cents.dummies.com** to register this book and tell us how you liked it!

- Get entered in our monthly prize giveaway.

- Give us feedback about this book — tell us what you like best, what you like least, or maybe what you'd like to ask the author and us to change!

- Let us know any other *...For Dummies®* topics that interest you.

Your feedback helps us determine what books to publish, tells us what coverage to add as we revise our books, and lets us know whether we're meeting your needs as a *...For Dummies* reader. You're our most valuable resource, and what you have to say is important to us!

Not on the Web yet? It's easy to get started with *Dummies 101®: The Internet For Windows® 98* or *The Internet For Dummies,® 5th Edition*, at local retailers everywhere.

Or let us know what you think by sending us a letter at the following address:

...For Dummies Book Registration
Dummies Press
7260 Shadeland Station, Suite 100
Indianapolis, IN 46256-3945
Fax 317-596-5498

BESTSELLING
BOOK SERIES
FROM IDG